UNDERSTANDING YOUR ANXIOUS CHILD

A PARENTS GUIDE TO HELPING KIDS OVERCOME THEIR FEARS AND ANXIETY TO LIVE A CAREFREE CHILDHOOD

ELIZABETH N. JACOBS

© Copyright 2021 - All rights reserved.

The content contained within this book may not be reproduced, duplicated or transmitted without direct written permission from the author or the publisher.

Under no circumstances will any blame or legal responsibility be held against the publisher, or author, for any damages, reparation, or monetary loss due to the information contained within this book. Either directly or indirectly. You are responsible for your own choices, actions, and results.

Legal Notice:

This book is copyright protected. This book is only for personal use. You cannot amend, distribute, sell, use, quote or paraphrase any part, or the content within this book, without the consent of the author or publisher.

Disclaimer Notice:

Please note the information contained within this document is for educational and entertainment purposes only. All eort has been executed to present accurate, up to date, and reliable, complete information. No warranties of any kind are declared or implied. Readers acknowledge that the author is not engaging in the rendering of legal, nancial, medical or professional advice. The content within this book has been derived from various sources. Please consult a licensed professional before attempting any techniques outlined in this book.

By reading this document, the reader agrees that under no circumstances is the author responsible for any losses, direct or indirect, which are incurred as a result of the use of the information contained within this document, including, but not limited to, — errors, omissions, or inaccuracies.

CONTENTS

Introduction — v

1. Understanding Anxiety — 1
2. The Goal — 35
3. Embracing the Truth about Anxiety — 58
4. Address Limiting Beliefs Early on and Develop New Belief Structures — 72
5. Healthy Alternatives — 93
6. Model Behavior — 122

Final Words — 137
About the Author — 147
References — 149

JUST FOR YOU FOR BUYING MY BOOK

A FREE GIFT TO MY READERS...

The 5 Day Challenge to Improving Communication

Anyone can implement this challenge right away and instantly start improving the relationships in their lives!

Visit the link:

Elizabethnjacobs.com

INTRODUCTION

"When you're feeling anxious remember that you're still you. You are not your anxiety."

— Deanna Reich

One of my best friends, I'll call her D., went through her entire childhood with a bad stomach. She cried at the mention of anything sad. If she saw a small puppy, she fell instantly in love with the dear thing, only to spend all night obsessing about the myriad of ways it might get hurt.

I met D. in grade school. We connected over our love of ponies and our shared distaste for math. It didn't take long for me to see how sensitive she was, how little it took for her to cry. One day a teacher's off-hand remark about her handwriting did her in, while another day, a friend's refusal to play with us had D. convinced she would never find love again.

Anxiety ruled her life and played a key role in our friendship. That all happened back in the late eighties and early nineties when no one talked about stress or depression in kids. My family often commented that I was a "sensitive thing" but didn't concern themselves too much with things like overly anxious children. My mother saw my good friend D. as overly dramatic, but no one ever used the word "anxiety" when discussing her issues.

D. became my constant companion, and I often observed her falling into a well of worries more often than not. It wasn't until I got into my teens that I started learning ways to calm myself down and then taught them to her. I also got into aerobics and dragged her to classes, positive the extra activity could stem her anxiety.

"Jump around more!" I'd insist. "You need it!"

She sometimes resisted, but most of the time she nodded a quick yes and got into the high-energy routines. We would sweat out our stress together, and she always told me to keep pushing her.

"It helps when you do it with me," she said once, so I always made sure I was her workout partner.

She listened, and together we created a routine that worked for both of us. I loved to go to bed early, but anytime D. came over she found it impossible to sleep. Together we'd try different soundscape CDs or chants to see what helped us drift off. She once told me she slept significantly better on my bedroom floor than in her bedroom, something I simply accepted. I didn't contribute her insomnia to the stress she faced at her own house.

As adults, D. and I discussed everything she faced as a little girl. The constant fighting and screaming at her house, hours by herself with no adult supervision, nights she went to bed hungry because she felt scared to put any of the Tupperware in the microwave.

In a lot of ways, D. was my living lab. She helped me learn how to take a step back and observe. I didn't help D. with any particular goal in mind. Instead, I threw out potential solutions with a "let us try it and see" approach. If what I did helped, I felt thrilled. If it backfired or did nothing, I learned to regroup, ask questions, and try again.

D. didn't get the therapy she desperately needed until later in her life. She struggled to find adults who took her problems seriously until she became a young adult herself. After she went to a few sessions with our college counselor, she met up with me for coffee.

"You know," she ventured, "going to therapy doesn't feel new for me."

"No?" I watched her, as I always did, waiting to see changes in her face.

She shook her head no and stared down into her latte. "Really, you've always been kind of like my therapist."

The comment struck me, but not enough to get me to change my major from Elementary Education to anything else. I graduated and made my way down the traditional path to teaching, but I never forgot what D. told me. Deep down, I thought my ability to listen to others and offer solutions could help me rise to new heights as a teacher.

My career path led to a few years of working with young children as a teacher and coach, a job I loved, but I found that I connected with kids in more of a counseling context.

Sitting and listening to students tell me their problems felt more important than anything taught in a classroom. How could anyone learn their multiplication or pass a spelling test if they felt the walls closing in on them?

I wanted to do more, so I continued my education by studying human relationships. I thought of all the little kids who so desperately wanted to just make friends and play, but couldn't stop the voices in their heads from mocking their every move. I thought of my young friend D, counting the minutes until she could sit in her room with a book and forget about everyone else's expectations of her for a few hours. How that was the only place she felt she could be herself.

After a lot of soul searching and long talks with friends, my partner, and student's parents, I turned part of my house into an office. I let all my former colleagues and room parents know I was open for business, eager to help.

You would not believe how many people called me up! I heard from stressed-out parents desperate for help to manage their emotions so they could then help their children. Tons of parents needed me to see their sons and daughters for a slew of issues. Some walked in with their entire family in tow for a group session.

I could see right away I'd made the right move. My generation grew up without the understanding of mental health we have today, and that lack of knowledge had endless repercussions. We all needed to find how to talk out our stress, our anxiety, our fears, and our regrets.

The journey started with my aim to help small children, but it quickly became apparent to me that moms and dads needed to be part of the process. If they couldn't model good emotion management, they couldn't talk to their children about how to do it, either. Parents felt left out entirely if kids came home with a new vocabulary about mental states, tools, or exercises.

So, I integrated everyone into the process and worked on everyone inside and out. I made sure parents understood that anxiety is something we all need, but we have to accept it, understand it, and manage it to become the best version of ourselves.

When a good friend suggested I write a book about my approach to anxiety to reach people beyond the walls of my office, I thought it sounded like a great idea.

That night I sat down and started the book you're reading now. I hope that together we can help shape the mental state you want for yourself and your child.

1

UNDERSTANDING ANXIETY

Before we get into how to manage anxiety, I want to clarify what I mean when I talk about anxiety as a mental health issue. We all get nervous from time to time, but some children experience anxiety at extreme levels.

Here's how it can present itself physically and emotionally.

What is anxiety?

Anxiety stems from the powerful fears we feel as toddlers. For example, a little girl might wail at the thought of Mom leaving the room, while a little boy could get plagued by nightmares about circus clowns. Of course, we all get scared by different things, but many of us leave those excessive worries behind as we learn more about the world and the real dangers it presents.

When we grow into our bodies and the world, we experience fears of all kinds. For example, we might get a sick feeling around a suspicious neighbor or worry about getting lost in an amusement park.

These fears grow from the seeds we plant in our minds as small children. A toddler's mother might leave and be late to pick her up from preschool, or a performer might be too intense or have disturbing makeup. Perhaps you have good reason to worry about that neighbor down the street.

As we get older, we either move past these fears and focus on things we enjoy, or we find we can't put these fears down. Instead of finding other things to worry about, those initial feelings of trepidation follow us around and refuse to be quiet. They morph and grow into a state of constant nervousness, imagined enemies, or irrational scenarios our minds convince us will happen one day.

For kids, this happens mainly in some common scenarios.

The first is separation anxiety - the fear that someone leaving will disappear and leave him all alone. It happens at night or when you need to leave your child at daycare or with a family member. Your child may not understand that you are leaving them for a set amount of time, not forever.

The second takes the form of extreme fear or phobia. We couldn't understand why my little nephew had a deep, intense fear of dogs. He'd grown up with dogs, yet he felt the need to run in the other direction if a dog barked at him or approached him in hopes of some affection. After talking to him, we understood it was the sight of a strange dog's teeth that set him off - he felt certain each dog wanted to bite him. Once we were able to pinpoint the why we were able to help curb that fear.

Social anxiety is the third scenario. This can affect kids as they attend school, go to church, or meet extended family. In their minds, everyone who can see them judges them endlessly and can't wait to embarrass them publicly. This can stem from an unpleasant experience with a stranger, hearing an offhand comment about themselves, or seeing something occur they feel certain will happen to them.

Social anxiety is crippling. It keeps kids out of school, derails friendships, and makes it that much harder to connect with anyone as an adult. Forget moving out of the house to go to college or start a job. A severe case of social anxiety can keep someone locked in her mind and her home for decades.

Finally, there's general anxiety. All the other styles stem from this overarching fear of the future. What will happen? When? Will I mess up? Will I be good enough?

Again, this is something we all feel to a degree, but some people feel it as a controlling force in their lives. They can't picture themselves in the future as confident and successful. Instead, they see a broken, failed person stumbling through the day and think, "That will be me. I'm certain."

All this anxiety takes a toll on our bodies, starting at a young age.

You might notice your child feels nervous about sleeping in her bed or has horrible nightmares regularly. In addition, she might always feel tired or irritable, have a consistently upset stomach, or constant headaches.

Some children experience an anxiety attack. This starts with a child struggling to take deep breaths and feeling his heart pound in his chest. He can then get dizzy and possibly faint. Anxiety attacks often get mistaken for heart problems because they make us feel our heart pound against our sternum. However, unlike a heart attack, an anxiety attack can be helped with deep breaths and some time away from the thing that spurred it.

Anxiety also affects a person's brain.

Anxiety in the brain

Beyond heart palpitations and the way our anxiety can stop us in our tracks, excess amounts of this emotion can also hurt our brain's anatomy. Anxiety keeps our brain from working normally, attacking in the four phases.

In a balanced, healthy brain, our hormones respond to stressful situations with Fight or Flight mode. That prepares our body to run from danger or face it head-on. To help us do that, cortisol and adrenaline hormones flood our nervous system to help us put up our dukes. Then, ideally, our sympathetic response can take over when the danger passes and help us return to a calm state of mind.

But out of control, anxiety keeps us from calming down. Instead, we stay in that stressed-out, overly aware state of mind and never quite make it back to tranquility. The excess cortisol and adrenaline make our anxiety grow with each negative experience. Our normal stress response ratchets up to a new level, as our mind now sees the world as endlessly dangerous.

Sometimes, our anxiety gets so high that the right side of our brains (where our imaginations live), is subject to huge beta waves, putting it out of balance with the left side. That means our excessive, made-up fears feel more and more real while our logical mind struggles to remind us we're caught up in emotion and not seeing the actual situation.

The section of our brain that sounds the alarm to alert us to danger is the amygdala. But anxiety with no checks or balances puts our amygdala on a hair-trigger, setting it off repeatedly. All that hyperactivity makes the amygdala bigger and more reactive, giving it more control than it should have.

Those cries of "Danger! Danger!" go straight to the hypothalamus, which tells our nervous system that we're under threat. Many people with extreme anxiety become hyper-reactive because their brains work overtime to make them overly aware of the surrounding environment. Every giggle suddenly becomes a critique of their appearance. Each glance is filled with disdain and judgment.

After months or years of this constant, internal attack, the brain starts to physically change and function differently than a calm brain. The mind's inner workings no longer benefit this person, but actively work against him.

All of this reworked sense of danger weakens the connection between the brain's prefrontal cortex and the amygdala. The prefrontal cortex holds our rational responses to the world. If it can't communicate with the amygdala, we lose our ability to see what's happening and instead replace reality with a living nightmare.

This weakened connection also makes solving problems or pursuing goals seem impossible.

Instead, we hide from bill collectors, insist we love our dead-end jobs, and avoid friendships or new experiences. As a result, an anxious person may turn to irrational solutions or erratic behavior in place of a clear, logical solution to their problems.

Finally, anxiety affects the hippocampus of the brain. The hippocampus stores our memories, but it shrinks as we feel stress. Like the prefrontal cortex, all this malfunction makes it weaker with each injection of adrenaline and cortisol. Soon, the misfires of the brain make it impossible for the hippocampus to store any memories beyond the worst of the worst.

You may notice that your child, or possibly you, tend to dwell on the worst parts of your past.

Perhaps you remember the lowest point of a day instead of the highlight. Maybe you had a great night out but can only fixate on a random, mean comment someone made about your outfit or that joke that didn't go over well, never mind the wonderful moments of the evening.

To summarize, anxiety affects the brain to the point it can no longer function normally. Instead of working as a logical thinking machine, the anxiety-riddled brain creates monsters and then convinces its owner those creatures are not imagined. They are real and waiting behind every corner.

Now the question every parent asks me - will this change the way my child learns?

Anxiety and learning development

Before I break down all the how and why, I want to confirm that yes, anxiety changes the way children learn. As I described in the last section, the prefrontal cortex of the brain normally grows throughout childhood. This helps children to be logical and control their emotions and impulses.

An anxious brain has a smaller prefrontal cortex, making logical thought much harder for kids.

Imagine trying to learn to read while your brain fights off lessons about phonics or punctuation in favor of fighting for our safety every second of every day. It's nearly impossible! The part of the brain that's meant to focus on learning from the teacher instead focuses on perceived threats, human or not, on all sides of the room.

This smaller logical section also makes solving social problems feel impossible. For example, anxious children may be more likely to get into a schoolyard fight, work for a bully's approval, or hide from the teachers or staff working to help them, all thanks to the smaller, weakened prefrontal cortex.

Physical symptoms of anxiety can keep kids out of school. For example, a bad stomach paired with a lack of sleep or stress headaches makes for more sick days than other kids. It can also kickstart several common ailments like a cold, stomach flu, or odd inflammation.

Essentially, anxiety makes for a kid who struggles on all fronts, especially in school.

Fear and biology

It's essential to understand the difference between fear and anxiety. Fear serves a biological purpose, while anxiety works entirely differently.

When we see a physical threat, such as a weapon aimed at us, something on fire, or a dangerous animal headed our way, we feel afraid. That burst of adrenaline helps us run away and find somewhere safe. Fear keeps us alive.

Fear gives us something author James Clear describes as an Immediate Return. We see our house is burning; we run for some water; the fire goes out; we feel better. The human brain is designed for Immediate Returns. That level of response kept us alive as a species, but now we've created an entirely unfamiliar environment.

In the modern world, we get what Clear calls a Delayed Return Environment. Over the past 500 years, our world became a place where we could stop and think about the future. However, we can't know for sure what our future will look like. We've moved beyond surviving lion attacks and burning huts. Now we have to think about our future as college students, moving up in our profession, and retirement.

This world of delayed returns works in direct opposition to our brain's requirement for immediate returns. The dissonance keeps us from feeling comfortable at all times, even when we can see that we have shelter, food, and water close by and no immediate threats.

Both humans and their fears have evolved and developed over the years, so we need to change our attitude about how we express anxiety and its role in our lives. But, there's good news - we can adjust how we tackle big problems by taking on small ones every day and working for those immediate returns.

But all of this begs an important question.

Why are today's kids so anxious?

I'll never forget the day my mother asked me, "Why do you only spend time with depressed or anxious people?"

The question stopped me in my tracks. "Mom," I said, my eyes wide, "I don't know anyone who isn't depressed or anxious!"

The two of us looked at one another the same way a human might stare at an alien fresh off the ship.

That two-sentence conversation showed us something imperative; our two generations deal with entirely different problems.

I would love to see younger patients live in a more loving, empathetic world, but they seem to be attacked from all sides with constant threats. Everything from Fear Of Missing Out (FOMO), that pops up whenever they don't get invited to a friend's house or a party to running for their lives when an active shooter breaks into their school. Add the constant state of being judged on social media and stressing over who likes them and why, then sprinkle in fear of watching the world burn soon, and it's a wonder anyone can calm down.

In 2015, the Ontario Student Drug Use and Health Survey (OSDUHS), spoke with over 10,000 students in grades 7 through 12. They found some disturbing results.

One major issue for kids is a lack of physical exercise. About one in five kids gets 60 minutes of vigorous activity a day, and that intense, sweaty movement helps lots of young people release that anxious feeling. Without it, all that nervous energy can build up and keep kids up all night or keep their thoughts spinning out of control.

Kids who don't get harmed at school constantly worry about it thanks to the prevalence of physical attacks at school and ongoing threats from cyberbullies. About half of teenagers hold after-school jobs, so they get to deal with work stress on top of everything else.

I had it rough growing up, we all did, but I am eternally grateful I got to live in a world without the internet in its current state. Sure, we had our problems, but listening to my young clients often blows my mind - these kids are getting put through the wringer!

What level of anxiety is "normal"?

I don't like to use the word normal, but I'll make an exception here in place of a description like "average" or "expected."

Normal fears develop with a child's age, but the hope is that they'll leave these developmental anxieties behind as our kids grow. Here's a quick breakdown of acceptable, normal fears you may see in your child.

Infants - In their first year, little ones fear people they don't know. It's a rational fear - we instinctively know that we need our parents to grow and develop. Who is this other person? Is she here to take me away? Mom, help!

This can manifest in a reluctance to be left at daycare, preschool, or hesitation to stay with a babysitter. Your child may cry, cling to you with all their might, or refuse to move away from you.

Toddlers - At ages one and two, kids get scared of strangers and of being left alone. Your child isn't comfortable on her own or with new people yet and might wail with fear once she realizes you're headed out the door.

As kids potty train, they can develop a fear of things like pooping (many fear it may hurt or that they'll get dirty if they do it), or falling into the toilet. In addition, many feel the pressure to get out of diapers and into big kid underwear, and that pressure can cause high amounts of anxiety.

. . .

Small children - In their first six years, kids can't always draw the line between real and imaginary things. A scary dream feels like an all too real memory. A loud noise becomes a monster under the house, and a strange shadow becomes a dark, persistent presence.

Lots of kids ask to sleep with their parents in hopes an adult can keep these boogeymen at bay. Parents often have explanations for what's happening, and logical discussions help little ones when they're scared of something they don't know or can't see.

Older children - Kids between 7 and 10 are learning about death, natural disasters, disease, and other real-world dangers. They understand the importance of good grades, so they realize a lousy test score can have long-term consequences.

At this age, kids have a new sense of strangers. They don't fear people they don't know unless they get a gut feeling an individual or a group of people can't be trusted. Unfortunately, social fears also build at this age, and many kids fear they may not have enough friends or that they don't fit in.

Preteens - The obvious fear at this age is puberty. Seeing their bodies change can terrify kids, particularly when they suspect they may be far ahead or way behind on their progress. They'll often compare their looks or actions to those of others and worry they don't measure up.

Public speaking fears appear at this age. Kids are expected to give presentations in class or perform in school plays, which leaves many preteens shaking in apprehension. In addition, social pressures ratchet up at this age as many sign up for social media and spend more time online.

How do we know when kids cross the line from an average amount of fear to a dangerous level?

Signs of anxiety

High levels of anxiety or extreme stress can express themselves in many ways, but I consistently see several things.

Before I give you this list, I want to encourage you to trust your parenting instincts. If you feel your child struggling, if you see a pained expression on his or her face, and if have the means and ability to do so, I suggest you schedule a session with a professional. Even if you've misjudged the situation, a therapist can help keep the lines of communication open between child and parent and help you understand why you're feeling anxious about your child.

Think of therapy as the equivalent of an oil change for your car. Even if it's running fine, you still take it to the shop every six months. It does no damage and helps you avoid any surprises. Regular check-ins with a mental health professional work much the same way, even if you're confident everything is humming along.

The following are symptoms of a child struggling with anxiety you should always take seriously:

Physical

- Headaches or stomach aches unrelated to a virus or infection
- Lack of appetite outside of the home
- Fear of using a school or public bathroom
- Makes restless movements (but is not diagnosed with ADHD)
- Gets shaky or sweaty in a high-stress situation
- Tense muscles in relaxed moments
- Insomnia or an inability to stay asleep all night

Emotional

- Tendency to cry

- Hypersensitivity
- An irritable disposition for no apparent reason
- Feels afraid of making any mistake, even a small one
- Susceptible to panic attacks or worries, they might have a panic attack
- Feels preoccupied about the distant future
- Drop-offs at school, daycare or a friend's house make them nervous
- A tendency to have nightmares about her loved ones passing away

Behavioral

- Always asks "What if..?" questions (What if our house gets blown away? What if you die? etc.)
- Avoids group activities at school or home
- Falls silent when asked to work with or play with others
- Begs to not be made to go to school
- Stays indoors during lunch or recess periods
- Prefers to avoid kid group activities like birthday parties or school events
- Constantly seeks approval from the adults in their life their friends

- Insists he/she "Can't do it!" for unclear reasons
- Has sudden meltdowns or unexpected tantrums

Recognizing anxiety in yourself

We know kids model behavior they see in their parents, but did you know kids learn all about stress and anxiety from us as well?

It's crucial that you take a hard look at yourself and how you manage your fears and anxieties about your life. You may believe you're putting on a brave face when in reality, all your emotional pain is on display.

I talked to one mother who insisted everything was "just fine!" and her son had no reason to avoid socializing with anyone.

"He quit soccer. He has one friend he only speaks to in a chat online," she told me while her son sat quietly in my toy corner. "He had a chance to join a chess club, and he practically ran the other way.

I don't know what to do!"

She put her head in her hands and took a breath. I put on my authoritative voice and asked her, "How often do you socialize with your friends or indulge in a hobby?"

The mom jerked her head up and said, "What? I don't have time for any of that!"

Unfortunately for this mother, her son saw her lack of social life as a sign that friends or acquaintances are not to be trusted. The two of them never discussed the ins and outs of friendship or why it was necessary. All the messages he received about interacting with others were her unspoken words.

I often find that kids who have high stress levels either have significantly stressed parents. This can result from single parenthood, a low income for the family, exposure to violent people, or a lack of consistency in some aspect of their lives.

There's good news for everyone - accepting our anxiety and understanding it feels incredibly empowering.

Step One: Seeing your anxiety

Before you can manage anxiety, you need to know what it looks like. Pay attention to how you see change or receive additional information. For example:

You get a raise. You think, "Oh no! The boss is going to expect twice as much work from me!" Or, you get a raise and think, "Awesome! I did it!"

We want the second reaction, but most of us choose the first. Why?

Anxiety likes to play tricks on us. It makes us nervous about new decisions, advancements, even steps forward in our career, like a raise or a promotion. That negative voice in our head tells us not to get too comfortable - good times now mean something terrible is on the way!

Instead of feeling accomplished and grateful, a red flag goes up. Somehow, things going our way make us scan the horizon. We expect to pay for this in some strange way, as if any success must be tempered with bad, ugly things.

Anxiety also makes us assign blame. Here's an example:

My heart is pounding, and I can barely breathe. I think I need to see a cardiologist! Or, my heart's going quick, and my breathing is shallow - I think I'm feeling anxious and need to deal with my emotions.

Again, which one sounds like you - option one or option two?

Option one is a typical response for most adults feeling ill. Rather than looking inside ourselves for the source of the problem, we look for any other cause. It's my heart. It's my job, and I have to get out of this town. It's because I don't eat enough kale!

We work very hard at avoiding our emotional state. I say we because even as a counselor, I do it too. Imagine if we put all that energy and effort into giving ourselves love, empathy, and time to care for our bodies.

Okay, last one.

Anxiety makes us feel behind the curve, or like we disappoint the surrounding people. It tells us, "Sure, you have a career, but look at Susan. She started her own business. You should do that, too."

There's no rule stating we all must run a small business, yet suddenly we feel terrible because we've failed to do something arbitrary, or we didn't do it soon enough, or we tried and we didn't make millions of dollars.

Anxiety loves the word should, telling us, "You should be thinner. Your skin should be smoother. You really shouldn't have cut your hair short - have left it long..." And on and on.

So here's my final test. When you see someone close to you, maybe a sibling or a friend, start earning a higher income, do you think -

"Wow! Good for her!" Or, "What? She's making that much money every year? I really should work harder..."

Of course, you can work harder, but you'll always find someone who earns more than you, is younger than you, fits into tinier jeans, or has one less wrinkle than you. You'll never run out of things you don't have.

Once you recognize your anxiety, you must own it and reshape your response.

Step Two: Changing your attitude about anxiety

Have you ever had someone see you on a bad day and say, "Jeez, calm down!" as if you had a switch to turn off your nerves?

Me too. And I hate it just as much as you do because I know from my studies and personal experience that this is the worst way to respond to a panic attack or heightened anxiety.

It's possible to get anxiety about anxiety. However, if each time we get anxious, we internally punish ourselves for having the nerve to feel anxious, we only perpetuate the problem. So instead, we have to see what our anxiety does for us and use it to our advantage.

Here are some mental exercises to practice to feel better about feeling anxious.

- Think of anxiety as a member of your internal family - You know all those different mental states you can have, like ecstatic happiness, your competitive side, or your state of complete relaxation? Anxiety is part of the crew, and she's going to visit from time to time. Put her on the same level as your other mental states and accept that you must experience anxiety as part of your emotional tapestry. She completes the picture.

- Remember that anxiety is a signal - When we feel anxious, it means our mind and body need love and empathy. Too much sitting still, mulling over something that we can't control, being too hard on ourselves can lead to high amounts of anxiety. It's like a fire alarm telling us to do something healthy. We need exercise, to journal, to focus on things we can control, and to feel grateful for the surrounding people.

- Don't label emotions as good or bad - I find this a lot in my female clients. We have many people around us who want us to have "good attitudes" or keep a smile on our faces. No one tells us sadness or anxiety is necessarily bad, but the signals are all around us. We think of some emotions as positive and others as negative. Remember, you need all of your emotions, and it's not your responsibility to make others happy all the time. If you need to leave the room to cry or sit in silence, that's what you need. No judgment.

- See your anxiety as a gift - Anxiety teaches us constantly. It can help us avoid high-stress situations, make us work a little harder, force us to leave our procrastination behind, or remind us to care for ourselves. In a lot of ways, anxiety enlightens us. If we can feel grateful for our anxiety and everything it shows us, we can appreciate our interactions with this intense, incredible emotion.

Step Three: Be aware of how you pass anxiety to others

Once you have a good handle on your anxiety, you can monitor how your stress affects your kids. Stress and anxiety can easily pass from one person to another, but certain techniques keep it contained.

First, calmly state how you're feeling. Avoid yelling, "I'm so freaked out!" or something similar, particularly in front of your children.

Kids learn how to navigate nuanced situations from the adults in their life. If we show them a version of ourselves that can't handle fear or anxiety, they'll remember it forever. So instead, try taking some deep breaths, counting to ten, or any technique that helps you feel a bit more grounded before you explain how you're feeling.

Then, say in a calm, respectful voice that you're feeling anxious, but that's okay. You know how to respond to those emotions.

Finally, ask for what you need. "Could I please have thirty minutes of quiet?" is a great request. It has a time limit, and it's considerate of the people in your home. Another option is, "I think I need some exercise. I'm going to put on a yoga video. You can join, but you're free to go play."

You'd be amazed what happens when we state, clearly and respectfully, what we need. It's a great alternative to "A moment of peace! I beg you!" or something along those lines.

Second, start a dialogue about emotions. I often tell parents to try this with puppets. I don't know the exact reason, but many people, especially adults, feel more comfortable talking about their internal turmoil through a fun, colorful character.

A straightforward talk over dinner is also great. Wait until the meal is over and talk about yourself first. Mention a low point in your day or something coming up soon that's making you sweat. If you tell a story first, then pause, your child will tell a story about how she feels.

Very young children might struggle with this. They don't have the patience to listen to a grown-up story. Instead, you can talk about emotions directly. Talk about what you feel, then give those emotions names, colors, temperatures, an animal classification, whatever your child enjoys. Then, in future conversations, you can ask if your little one feels like a purple dinosaur.

Keeping the dialogue about emotions open takes the negative charge out of sadness or fear. Be sure to use the same descriptions as your child to describe your feelings, talk about how you manage them, and reinforce the importance of good habits.

Finally, take care of yourself. I know self-care can be a challenge for a lot of parents. We don't all have time to go to the gym, soak in a bathtub or run away to the mountains for a Buddhist retreat.

But self-care can be one small thing you do for yourself every morning.

Take five minutes to meditate before you start work. Put on a short, freebie workout video and get your blood pumping. Make a healthy meal for dinner. If you can get away for a walk in the park, sit and journal about your concerns, or join a friend for coffee, make it a priority. Please don't wait until you have time; put it on your calendar. Those moments can make a world of difference.

Finally, know when to disengage. You want to use your best judgment about when to let your stress show around your family and when to experience it yourself. Does having an emotional reaction to school drop-offs help your kids understand how to manage stress or simply stress them out?

I want you to have good strategies to manage your stress and be open about how you feel, but a big part of being the adult in the room is knowing when to step out.

Stay one step ahead

Anxiety resembles a small, unattended fire. If we add fuel, soon we have a roaring blaze too out of control to put out. Like fire, anxiety feeds on anxiety and makes us nervous the more we expose ourselves to it. It's hot, sweaty, and incredibly alarming.

Just like firefighters, we can put anxiety to a stop before it starts. Instead of waiting until that blaze is melting the ceiling, we can stomp out the sparks.

Here are a few daily things you can do to help keep your anxiety from burning down your sense of well-being.

Focus on deep breathing

One of the best pieces of advice I have yet to receive about moments when I feel anxious is to focus on how my body feels, not what I'm thinking. It's an excellent way to stop the high-speed carousel of thoughts from spinning out of control.

Whenever I lose myself in old, negative memories, regrets, or a slew of worries, I reach out and touch something. It can be a tree, the shower wall, anything to ground me. Then I breathe.

The trick to a calming breath is to count. Start by breathing in for four breaths, then out for four. I know it's a low number, but it's attainable and easy to remember. Let your breath bring your attention back to your body and away from your mind. Focus on how you feel.

Don't judge how you're feeling. If you ate too big of breakfast or under-slept, don't chastise yourself for not being a health nut. Instead, notice the feeling; give it your attention. If you don't like the way you feel, set a goal for changing your habit of eating deep-fried or greasy food or let your family know you need to go to bed an hour earlier.

You can try several breathing exercises, but here's my favorite.

Get comfortable in a chair or lying down, then take your left index finger and close your left nostril. Next, relax into your sitting or supine position, and breathe slowly, in and out, for two minutes.

Our breath functions like the brake pedals of the brain; therefore, this exercise gives the brain a compassionate slowdown. Anytime I feel overwhelmed, this quick practice changes my state of mind in a mere two minutes. It's magic.

Exercise

I know not everyone has time to get to the gym or go for a run but remember, prioritize your workout yourself. If you don't demand that time, don't expect to get it.

See if there's a nearby class, space, or swimming pool you can use at least three times a week. Make sure it's within your budget! Please don't go broke signing up for an expensive gym if you can find a reasonable alternative.

I use a workout app that gives me daily reminders to do a thirty-minute workout and a five-minute meditation every morning. Best of all, it's free! There are tons of yoga YouTube channels, accessible apps, and lots of cheap, online classes you can check out if you like to work out at home.

If you can't get motivated on your own, let your friends and family know you're looking for a workout buddy. First, you need someone at or slightly above your level and who has a schedule that works with yours. Then, you need to coordinate some type of workout in the park, running through the neighborhood, or at a nearby public space.

Don't forget to check nearby community centers, go online and look for aspiring yoga or pilates teachers who want to lead a small, local class, anything that might be beneficial to you and the people around you. You never know where you might find a free workout!

Also, keep an eye out for any brand new gyms or workout studios. A lot of new spaces give their first customers great deals. I once got a VIP membership to a little yoga studio for $50 because they wanted to up their numbers that year. I could drop in whenever I needed an hour of mindful exercise with a deep meditation afterward.

Exercise is a great way to get back into your body. It takes a lot of the tension out of your body and gives you a chance to be a primal, sweaty being for an hour. Aim for three good workouts a week, then walk or run when you can between workout days.

If you struggle with extreme anxiety, consider a high-impact, fast-paced workout. I love trampoline class, a Latin rhythms workout, or boxing. If your anxiety feels out of control, you can rein it in with some intense, sweaty exercise.

Revisit your budget

It's difficult to score a high-paying job or client who recognizes your worth and pays you accordingly. Most of us have to make do with what we have, and that's okay! The important thing is to go into the world with a clear vision of what you can afford and how often.

A few years ago, I worked with a lovely gentleman who was a bookkeeper for several local businesses. When I mentioned to him I struggled to budget, he assured me anyone could do it.

"What most people don't realize," he told me, "is that money has to be thought of as a two-ended organism. When money comes in, that's a credit. When it goes out, that's a debit. So if you can track both things, you can balance a budget."

He suggested a few different videos and free, downloadable templates to help me keep track of what I earned and what I spent. To my complete shock, I got the hang of it almost instantly. Now I encourage all of the adults I work with struggling with anxiety to do the same.

When we feel in control of our finances, we can take a massive bite out of the anxiety that plagues us. It's also incredibly empowering - living within my means, canceling any extra monthly costs that ate away at my bank account, and earmarking my money for specific purchases felt great. I never knew managing money could be such a significant step forward!

Take care of yourself

I'm going to talk a lot about self-care in this book. You must take care of yourself, so your child has a clear idea of what self-care looks like and understands the value of putting their well-being first.

I know a lot of parents who struggle to take a day to do all the things they need to do - meditate, exercise, write in a journal, visit a therapist, spend some time with nature - whatever helps them feel their best. Yet, despite the thousands of benefits, they feel they somehow aren't allowed to do this.

I always tell these reluctant moms and dads the same thing - if you decide to take care of yourself now, your kids won't have to take care of you in the hospital or from your bed. I tell them to think of it as recharging a phone. You don't ask your phone to run constantly as its battery runs out. So why should we ask ourselves to keep running and running when our batteries are at one percent?

I think the best thing to do with your family is to sit everyone down and tell them what you need. Don't ask permission, don't apologize, state it as a fact.

"I need to manage my stress and anxiety, so once a month I'm going to take a day off. You can't call me, you can't come with me, it's a day for me. I promise to be home by (name a time), and I will be Mommy/Daddy again but not before. I know this is hard for everyone, but if I don't do this, I'm going to become very unhealthy and anxious."

Once you have your day lined up, you can do whatever you like. I only ask that you minimize time in front of a screen. I understand catching up on shows is sometimes a treat, but this exercise is designed to get you away from the house! Take yourself out to a movie theater, lunch, a walk in the park, anything you want. Be careful, and keep phone use to a minimum and leave the laptop at home.

Instead, plan and let your boss or clients know this is a mental health day and that you'll be back online the following day. Remember, it's rare for anyone to email an emergency. Most of our messages can wait 24 hours or more.

Finally, talk about how much better you feel after you've prioritized your well-being, how nice it feels to meditate after a session of exercise, and how great the park was that day. Let your kids hear about a positive experience you had, so they mimic you.

Kids take in what we say, but they mimic what we do. Take on your anxiety so your children follow suit.

2

THE GOAL

We don't want to eliminate, but to understand the anxiety

There's a reason so many of us struggle with anxiety; it's a brain function we all share. Anxiety can be a friend, but only if we use it properly.

How can anxiety work for your child, not against him? How can we turn the dialogue about anxiety into something positive that everyone feels comfortable discussing?

First, we need to see anxiety as a part of our human experience, not a disease in need of a cure.

Anxiety does a lot of great things for us - it makes us aware of unseen, vague threats, it gives us an internal tug when we get close to someone who might not be good for us, it lets us know when we need to rethink a decision.

Second, we have to appreciate and thank this part of our brain function. And third, we need to make it work for us.

Let's dive in and discover how to take this transformative journey.

Let your anxiety be, but don't let it take control

It might sound like I'm telling you to simply be anxious and leave it alone, but I assure you that's not what I want. Instead, I want you and your child to understand that anxiety can't be drugged or meditated away. No matter what we do, anxiety continues to live inside us. How we build a relationship with it and relate to it can change how we live our lives.

The opposite end of the anxiety spectrum is an extreme complacency, a reluctance to do or feel anything. But somewhere in between constant, intense fear and complete apathy is a state we call mindfulness or living in the moment. That's the realistic goal.

So, how to make our way to the middle?

You can start by understanding anxiety. It's contagious. We can pick it up from a stressed-out boss who's disrespectful or freaked out about a prominent contractor who can't manage his or her stress very well. Also, it feeds itself. If we dwell too much on fear, then lock into our anxiety around that fear, that horrible sense of impending doom becomes too big to manage.

Then, we have to work to see patterns in our actions. A journal, even a quick voice note about how you feel each day, can help with this. Check in with your kids on their feelings, too. Note down if there are days they feel more anxious than others if certain activities make them jittery or help them relax.

Remember not to judge any actions or make suggestions at this stage. We want to start with a clear record of observations—nothing else.

Another thing I want you to notice is the time you or your children spend on social media. Seeing images of others' successes in life or just gatherings that never have your face in them can enhance that feeling of getting left behind, forgotten. Also, posting something in hopes of thousands of likes or shares only to be ignored or getting negative comments can eat away at our mental health.

A lot of young people see their online status as somehow more real than their real-life interactions. Make sure you and your children limit your social media time (or get your family off social media entirely), to keep those feelings of isolation in check. Again, journal about how it feels to let that digital interaction go and its effect later on.

After you have some solid observations, talk to your kids about things that make you anxious. Don't ask them questions about their anxiety (that comes later). Instead, let them know they're not alone in their struggles.

If your kids open up and tell you a story about an intimidating classmate or their fears around unique life events, just listen. Don't offer a solution or judge their decision to stay away from certain situations. Remember, their brain is trying to keep them safe, just like yours. Instead of saying, "Here's how to handle that..." try, "That sounds tough. Thanks for telling me what happened."

It sounds odd to stop being the guiding hand in our children's lives, but I promise it helps. Thanking your son or daughter for sharing sends a great message. *I'm not here to judge you. I'm here to help.*

If your child asks for advice or for you to intervene, then go ahead. Otherwise, focus on building compassion. I promise you'll get it back in kind.

Speaking of help, it's time to practice getting uncomfortable.

A great soft skill that many people lack is the ability to navigate an uncomfortable situation. We hear a lot about emotional intelligence, spatial reasoning, a friend who can remember anyone's name, but it's rare we praise someone for being able to sit in discomfort.

Believe it or not, this is an important life skill. Anyone who wants to manage a staff has to make his or her peace with confronting a poor worker or someone acting inappropriately. These are painful conversations, but if we want our workers to respect us and focus on getting their jobs done, we have to have them. End of story.

You can practice feeling uncomfortable with your child. Here are a few things you can try in public places.

- Sit or lie down on the ground for three minutes in a public place with a lot of foot traffic. Try to be as much of an obstacle as possible without putting yourself in danger.

- Approach a stranger (together), in a park or cafe and ask them about something they're doing or wearing. Try to keep the conversation going for at least two minutes.

- Try climbing a tree or going up an outdoor staircase as high as you can and then down again in full view of strangers.

- Wave to someone you don't know and see if you can get him or her to wave back.

Whenever you practice being uncomfortable with your child, take the time to reflect on the experience afterward. Talk about how you felt versus what physically happened. Maybe the two of you felt mortified to sit on the ground at a metro station while people rushed past you, but did anyone do anything? Did you get confronted?

People in public are often overly polite. You'll rarely have someone scream at you for sitting down or saying hello, yet we often feel that we'll get an earful if we try one of these things. We have to go through with it to show ourselves that it won't happen.

I once took a camera to a small town craft fair and walked through with my friend. I wanted to get pictures of the crowd, the stands, and some creations. But my friend felt confident we'd get kicked out.

"The artists are all going to think you're stealing their ideas!" she hissed in my ear. I looked around to see if anyone seemed hostile to the amateur photographer snapping pictures, but no one seemed to mind.

"You're being silly," I told her and went on getting shots here and there. She went into a total panic, wrung her hands, and waited for us to get shown the door or shamed publicly. I asked her to stand under a taxidermied eagle posed with its wings wide open. She agreed, but only after glancing around like a criminal to make sure the coast was clear.

Later, when I looked at the photo, her face looked paper-white, and her eyes bugged out in terror. Where I'd practiced feeling uncomfortable, she had none. And it showed.

More practices to do with your kids

Aside from practicing and getting okay with discomfort, there are plenty of things you can do to help an anxious child in his daily routine.

- Practice deep breathing - Encourage your little one to slow down, take deep breaths, count to ten, anything neutral that brings him back to the present. Try deep breathing while shuffling playing cards, listening to relaxing music, or singing a favorite song.

- Try chunking - Chunking is the practice of breaking an extensive project or presentation into small steps. Take a child's worry or fear and turn it into minor challenges. If your child fears social gatherings, start by watching groups of kids play together. Then, try inviting over one or two children the same age as your son or daughter. Eventually, build up to a bigger group or party.

- Schedule worry time - Make one part of your child's day a chance to write or draw pictures of things that scare them or make them feel stressed. You can put everything into a box or hang them all on a wall. Set a timer to show that worrying needs to stop when the clock runs out. After worry time, close the box and put it away or tear down all the worries off the wall and poof! They're gone.

- Keep it positive - Try using basic strategies to avoid a negative mindset. If your child seems anxious, mention that he looks "excited". If your child gets hung up on different scenarios that may arise, remind him he has already been in certain situations and that he has handled it well. Or, use evidence to thwart unrealistic fears like scary clowns prowling around at night (clowns are just people wearing a lot of makeup). You can also plan out how to handle different situations that may happen during a school day or a day out.

- Emphasize having fun - Parents sometimes overtly or accidentally pressure kids to win or be perfect. It's normal; we all want the best for our children. But you can sidestep this by focusing on the goal of having a good time, making a reasonable effort, or making new friends. Try saying things like, "Find a way to make your book report fun," or "Enjoy the race!"

- Verbalize your fears - If you ever feel hesitant to do something new or talk to someone, say something about it to your child. Try, "You know, I think the author is so cool. I'm a little scared, but I'm going to say hi when I go to her book reading."

- Build a sense of control - If your kids worry about lions stalking the front yard, make lion patrol a part of your evening ritual. Send them outside to see firsthand that no dangerous animals are strolling through your lawn. Give them special equipment like a new flashlight, a reflective vest, a pair of boots, anything that helps your kids feel brave. Then send them out on their own and let them report back to you. Ask your kids to lock the doors and check the window latches before bed can also help them feel safe at night.

- Be honest - Images on TV or the internet depicting war, violence, or famine can deeply disturb some children. If your son or daughter comes to you with concern on their face, speak openly about some of the bad things in the world. Sugarcoating the real world can often backfire (kids are great lie detectors), and make you seem untrustworthy. After you talk frankly about what's happening in the world, remind your child that they are safe, surrounded by people who love them. You can also help look for a foundation or effort to help people affected by a recent crisis.

- Look for outside help - Extreme anxiety can keep kids from leading happy, full lives. If you're concerned your child isn't taking part in fun activities or suffering in school because of anxiety, seek a family-based program that can help. A great example is Australia's program BRAVE.

- Take a step back - Finally, make sure you aren't overly protective. If you hover over your child at homework time, you may accidentally send a negative message - "you'll never get this done on your own." Or, if you stay close when it's time to play with a worried look on your face, your daughter may see that as a sign that others aren't to be trusted. Check your habits and do your best to show your child that it's okay to take a risk.

Manage fear

We all have to face our fears eventually, but we've also all had that person in our life who pushed us a bit too far. When I begged my mother not to make me swim in the deep end of the public pool (the water was pitch dark and made my heart race), she scoffed and insisted. I know she had good intentions, but I had nightmares for years.

So, what's the right way to get a child over their fears?

Gradual, tiny steps

Imagine your daughter is terrified of Santa Claus. No big deal, right? Santa's only in town for a limited time, and you can usually predict where he'll be.

But, what happens if an airport Santa is wandering around? Or if someone hires a Santa Claus for a family party?

Rather than be surprised and left with a screeching, traumatized child, it's better to prepare.

With the terrifying Santa Claus, you can use gradual exposure. Start by finding a spot near Santa Land where you can see Santa from a distance. Sit with your child and explain that you won't go any closer; you're going to watch the other kids, nothing else. Stay for about five minutes, then walk away and get a treat.

Next time, get closer. Maybe stand just beyond the display and watch again. Talk about what Santa's doing, what the kids are doing, why kids like Santa. Focus on what's happening at the moment. If your child asks "What ifs," redirect the conversation to what she can see at the moment.

Do this little by little. Patience is key.

Be ready to go through it again and again

If your child isn't ready to approach Santa after a few observations, don't insist. Instead, practice deep breathing, write your worries and hold hands. Share a story of a time you had a pleasant visit with Santa. Read a story about a kind Santa Claus leaving toys at a house.

Try to use whatever you can to help your child get her anxiety down. Remember, shoving your kid up to a giant red Santa will only reinforce the fear.

Instead, try listening with compassion.

Practice empathy

Do your best to understand what exactly your child

fears. Listen to him describe what he is feeling and why. Then, try to feel it.

Empathy is an incredibly powerful tool for parents. Sympathy is nice, but it doesn't put us at the moment the way empathy can. Think of it as seeing someone down in a shallow pit feeling so sad he can't climb out.

A sympathetic response is to say, "Gosh, you're in a pit! I'm so sorry," then walking away.

The empathetic response is to climb down into the pit to sit with him and feel the cold, dark space, to really feel why he's there. Then, you can gradually help him out.

Get a pro

Family therapy can help your child manage his anxiety on a deeper, more lasting level. I understand therapy isn't always an option for budgets or time, but do your best to get any anxious child to a therapist, psychiatrist, or counselor once a week. That space is his safe space to get out all the things bothering him.

For very young children, you can look for a play therapist or art therapy. Older kids can also try teletherapy or therapy via video chats or texts.

No matter what you do, encourage your child to be open and have fun in session. You want him to know that therapy is his time; no one will judge what happens there.

Use your words

How much do our words, actions, or facial expressions change how others feel? Quite a lot, it turns out!

Many people in the world identify as Highly Sensitive People (or HSP), meaning they're empathetic to a fault. If someone in the room feels angry or upset, an HSP will take on that emotion. No context necessary.

That's why parents need to become highly reflective and aware of the words they say, their stance, facial expression. Once we look exasperated or terrified, a sensitive child can absorb all of that emotion.

Let's break down how to manage fears and be sure not to transmit our own worries into the heads of our sons and daughters.

Your own stress

If you suffer from high stress from work, your living situation, or something beyond your control, focus on what you can control. Many of the kids I work with have parents who are much more stressed than they realize. Some are so accustomed to a non-stop lifestyle they can't imagine slowing down.

When our children hear us make negative comments about people or events at work, it seeps into their subconscious. Remember, you can vent about work but think about the power your words have on the surrounding people. If you call your boss stupid or gripe about someone else getting a big client over you, your kids are listening.

Here's how you can rephrase some of your worries.

"I'm sad about something my boss said today. I need to find something fun to do so I don't dwell on it."

"I'm thrilled for X getting that big client, but I wish I could have been part of that project. Maybe I should start a new, fun hobby for myself at home."

You're still saying what's bothering you, but also acknowledging that the way you feel requires attention.

Avoid leading questions

A leading question is something that guides someone to the answer you want. For example:

"Can you please just admit that you ate the last of the ice cream?" differs from, "Any chance we have more ice cream in the freezer?"

You can see that one has a predetermined answer while the other is neutral. With anxious kids, we need to avoid -

"Do you feel nervous?" or "Are you scared?"

Instead, try, "How are you feeling right now?" or "Are you feeling anxious or are you feeling excited?"

The A/B question is an excellent way to get an honest answer out of kids. A simple "How do you feel?" is good to ask now and then, but not too often. Also, remember to listen with empathy whenever your child wants to share with you. Save the judgment for people you don't know!

Avoid anticipation

Anticipatory fear is fear that builds over long periods. Stressing over an upcoming exam, dreading a long flight, stressing over finally meeting our partner's parents can cause anticipatory fears.

For younger kids, the best thing to do is keep the anticipation to a minimum. Don't announce a "big surprise" weeks in advance. Instead, focus on keeping things calm and positive for six days, then let him or her know that something new is happening the next day.

Always give as much information as you can (who, what, when, where, why), and consider if surprises or significant changes are a good idea. If your child suffers from panic attacks, a massive change or a surprise birthday party could do her in. Instead, focus on sharing facts, keeping a planner just for her, or keeping a big calendar in a shared space so everyone can see what's coming up.

But don't avoid activities

Sure, anticipation can cause problems, but so can shutting down completely. You don't want to never have your child swim because he or she feels nervous at the pool.

Remember all the tactics we discussed. Break each challenge down into manageable mini-challenges. Sit next to the pool in a swimsuit, stand in the shallow end, and gradually jump into the water.

Practice deep breathing. You can do a family meditation, a basic set of deep breaths in the car, and do single-nostril breaths for two minutes.

Express feelings and fears during Worry Time. Remember to lock them up in a box, tear them down off the wall, or crumble them up and throw them in the garbage after you finish.

Ensure your child gets exercise for at least 60 minutes each day and plenty of sleep at night.

Then, when it comes time to swim, don't insist. Tell your daughter the times you'll go to the pool together. Explain no one will ever force her into the water, but everyone is there to help if she wants to try getting in. Everyone's there to have fun and enjoy the day. No one wants to judge how she looks, swims, or plays.

Once you get those basics into your daily routines, you can embrace anxiety.

Own your story

It's strange, but the moment we embrace the things we fear about ourselves is the exact second that thing loses its power. Something about fighting our anger or trepidations seems to feed them. Once we stop battling those things and start embracing them, suddenly, we're in control.

So what does that look like and sound like?

First, we have to say it out loud. "I'm an anxious person, so I need..." or "I use breathing exercises to help me manage my anxiety."

Giving a name to something that feels dark and hidden brings it out into the light. That thing stops being a boogeyman and takes the shape of an old friend. Now we can converse with it and walk with it, no more hiding.

Second, we can seek other people who share our experiences. For your child, that might mean hanging out with some kids who also get freaked out by the public pool and prefer to stay in and play board games. However, it also means finding friends who can express empathy when your little one says, "I'm scared."

Help your child find friends who don't encourage or build up their fear, but accept that this new friend is sensitive and won't just cannonball into the water like some kids.

A mix of both groups helps your child feel less alone, yet also reminds him to keep working on pushing boundaries and leaving their comfort zone (if only for a short time).

The combination of the two makes for a balanced, supportive experience. If your child can talk about his anxiety, it's no longer a point of shame. That vulnerability can lead to new friendships and help him find a community of kids with similar issues and others who can help them feel more confident.

. . .

Conversations with yourself

Anxiety likes to lie to us. It tells us we're bad people, a waste of space, someone who deserves less than nothing. Unfortunately, these harmful thoughts often become self-judgments kids express out loud. When no one disagrees with a comment like "I'm so ugly" or "I'm the worst swimmer in my group," many kids take that as confirmation. No one disagreed with me because I'm right.

Of course, it's important not to jump into compliment mode every time you hear these comments. Instead, talk about how that feeling of unattractiveness or failure came from an experience. Sure, maybe someone at school is better looking than you, but that's fine! Life is not a beauty contest.

And you may struggle in swim class, but guess what? You have a fantastic coach and plenty of time to get better.

Instead of insisting that your child is gorgeous or a swimming genius, ask him or her about these standards they've set for themselves. Why the sudden interest in their appearance? Did something happen at school? Why the stress over their swimming ability?

Pay attention to the events that caused these comments and the emotions they sparked. Make sure your child knows you don't expect perfection.

You can model this in your actions. Talk to your kids about things you want to do but aren't confident you can do well. Maybe you want to sing in public or draw a portrait. Let them see you try to then review your progress. Ask them to give you notes.

After a few days (or weeks), of going for your own goal, ask them what they saw. They'll likely tell you something like, "Mommy, you're not a singer." Explain to them that you're not a professional vocalist, but that's not why you wanted to perform. You set a goal because you wanted to express yourself and entertain your friends or that you just like to try new things.

When your child sees you or your partner learning and growing while never attempting to achieve perfection, it helps them understand a lot about the world. Perfection is subjective and changes from person to person. Enjoyment, laughter, learning - those are universal things, and we all need them in our lives.

Free yourself and others from judgment

The author Tara Brach writes about a great thing called loving-kindness. For adults, she recommends a mantra (a repeated phrase(s) that creates a sensation of love from the inside out. It starts with statements wishing for what we want:

"May I be healthy, may I be calm, may I be at peace..."

Her meditation guide encourages us to do this for two minutes a day and then increases the time little by little as we get better at settling into meditation. Then, we can add the next phase, sending out those good thoughts to other people.

"May you be healthy, may you be calm, may you be at peace..."

Finally, after practicing those two stages, we add the third phase, "You and I."

"May you and I be healthy. May you and I be calm..."

And so on. This is a great practice because it helps us focus on accepting ourselves first, then shifting that love and appreciation we feel inside to those around us. We don't have to forgive anyone or relive any past slights; we only wish good things for each other.

Meditations like this one can change our perception of the entire world. But what I love about it is how it makes us come to terms with how much we judge ourselves and each other.

Externalized judgments can feel harmless, but we need to keep in mind that if our children perceive us as judgmental, they'll put more pressure on themselves to meet our standards. An offhand comment like, "That security guard is terrible at his job!" can do a lot of damage when young ears hear it.

Try to temper your statements and ask questions if you can. Sure, some people are inept, but many of them simply had a bad day before you arrived. It's impossible to know the entire story in a brief exchange, so say that.

"That security guard seemed off today. I wonder if maybe something happened."

Let your child hear you make statements expressing curiosity, not judgment, to let him know you want to learn more about a situation. A poor grade or failed track meet won't be the end of the world. Instead, it's a chance to talk more about what happened and why, and how you'll tackle the next challenge together.

3

EMBRACING THE TRUTH ABOUT ANXIETY

I will never forget the time I avoided a water bill for over a year. I don't know why exactly, but one city's water company kept giving me free water. They'd send a long, confusing bill once in a while, and I'd try to make heads or tails of it, but inevitably I'd throw it out.

It seemed like a done deal - some secretary made a mistake and forgot to mark me down as UNPAID. But none of us can outrun the consequences of our actions. Not long after I moved out of that apartment, I got angry phone calls from my former landlady.

"What are these bills? Did you not pay for the water? Why didn't you pay?" and on and on. The municipal water system made sure the new tenant didn't get a drop of water until I paid my debt. I felt terrible, but I also felt ridiculous.

Whatever made me believe I could get away with evading bills for all those months?

We can't evade anxiety

Anxiety often works like an unpaid bill or an angry landlord. It refuses to be denied. The debt must be paid.

I often read articles about overcoming or "letting go" of anxiety, as if this part of our brains can simply be wiped away. If only it were that simple.

The more we deny it, the stronger our anxiety can grow. We've got to face and deal with it; the sooner the better, so it can't nestle into our subconscious and grow to insane proportions while we aren't looking.

So, what can we do?

First, we accept that anxiety will always be with us. So will happiness, sadness, boredom, all the rest. Yes, unchecked fears can harm, but we have many ways to manage our anxiety and show our children how to manage theirs.

Talk to your kids about how anxiety is a reality, not a condition or an illness. It's perfectly okay to be anxious. Everyone feels that way sometimes. Their anxiety doesn't set them apart; it makes them part of a community.

It's essential to erase the shame or embarrassment around anxiety. A lot of us feel anxious about being anxious. After a panic attack, for example, a young child or teen might stress over having their next attack, thus bringing it on faster. We need to present anxiety as something that occurs, not something that rules our lives.

Focus on the feeling

Anxiety can help us read our feelings. Like that unpaid bill, it wants our attention.

Any time your child mentions she feels anxious, ask them to close their eyes and focus on that feeling. Where is the body? It could occur in the chest, at the top of their head, in the stomach. Then give her a moment to really get to know that feeling.

After a few minutes, get her to do some deep breaths and see if she can feel that sensation drift away. If it doesn't, don't worry - there's something unspoken that needs their attention. Your child may need to draw out a concern or journal for a bit.

Very young children won't be able to identify how they're feeling right away. You'll have to look for cues in their behavior to know if your child is sad, angry, or frustrated. Then, you need to teach him or her the name of that feeling.

To help, have your child look at pictures of characters in books or observe other boys and girls in public. Ask him, "How is that little boy feeling right now? And that girl? Why do you think she has that look on her face?"

Once we can recognize and name an emotion, we defang it. Familiar things or feelings with names are far less scary than the unknown. After your child gets to know his or her feelings, you can assign each feeling a color or name to practice speaking openly about emotions.

This practice helps remind all of us (you included), that stress and worry can come and go. Our awareness stays with us at all times.

Reflect on reactions

No one gets their stress management right the first time. Instead of trying to be calm and perfect from the beginning, remind yourself that you're a work in progress, just like your son or daughter.

When you sit down to dinner or to get out your worries, think back to your day. What part of your day was the most stress or anxiety-inducing? How did you respond to that feeling?

Remember, no judgment! Instead, remember how you managed the sense of anxiety and reflect on how you felt afterward. Did you lash out at someone or retreat to your desk and refuse to confront the issue? Did you calmly approach the person causing the problem or go to HR?

None of these responses are wrong! If you lashed out, it's likely because you felt incredibly upset.

Yes, you owe the victim of your wrath an apology, but you need to acknowledge if those harsh phrases helped anyone. Hey, maybe that jerk had it coming. Or perhaps the better option was a calm chat. You tell me.

Ask your children to share (after you), and see how they feel about their reactions. My little nephew "let out a dinosaur roar" at some boys teasing him at school. When I asked him how he felt about it, he assured me he felt great.

It's an unusual solution, but it worked for him.

Own who you are

You can always verbalize your tendency towards stress or your anxiety. Saying "I'm an overly anxious person," or "I get nervous" is good practice. Make sure not to add any backpedaling like, "Sorry, but I'm anxious." You don't need to apologize for your feelings.

Let your child hear you say it, too. If you can own up to it, they won't struggle to hide their feelings but discuss them. Whenever you describe your child as anxious, frame it positively.

Avoid phrases like - "Matthew gets so anxious whenever he sees the neighbor's dog. It's a Pomeranian for goodness' sake!"

Instead, try - "Matthew gets nervous around dogs. We need to be respectful of his need for space and show him the neighbor's Pomeranian isn't dangerous."

It may take time, but your child will eventually own his anxiety. This is an important step.

Again, fighting that tendency towards nervousness or holding stress in poor light will only help it grow.

Saying "I have anxiety" can be a major game changer! When you hear your son or daughter express their anxiety, respond with something positive. Try, "Yes, I know. But I also know that you have some excellent techniques for managing your anxiety. You're very responsible."

That's empowerment.

Perfectionism

So many of the children I meet think the world needs them to fit an exact mold. They must be tall, have hundreds of friends, ride horses, swim with the champions. Kids get these ideas from several sources, but a major one is home.

The way we see success portrayed on television and online can make us internalize that expectation. No matter what, we must be rich, thin, beautiful, and eternally young. Though it is getting better, we rarely see a celebration of a low-income lifestyle or the joy of body acceptance. It's only recently movies, and tv highlighted problems or milestones unique to the elderly.

When we don't earn those millions of dollars or maintain a tiny waistline, we can beat ourselves up. Not intentionally or verbally, but by accident and in the deepest, darkest chambers of our heart. One little girl I worked with had trouble keeping her weight down. After seeing her mother train for a marathon and get into formidable shape, the poor dear felt certain her parents saw her as a chubby black sheep.

"Mommy isn't big," she told me. "Why am I?"

We had long talks about how everybody has their strengths. Her mother had a good build for long, punishing runs, but that didn't mean her daughter had to have the same one. This little girl loved being in the school play where she got to sing and dance.

"Plays need actors with all different shapes. Otherwise, how would we know who's who in the story?"

I also pointed out to her she took after her father - and she adored her father. Together we set some new standards - to continue auditioning for school plays, keep singing and dancing, and have fun with her theater friends. Those were standards she could easily meet.

Once met, she felt free to enjoy herself and stop stressing over how much she weighed. I spoke with her parents about her feelings about her weight, and her mother talked about how running made her happy and the people she ran with in the park. She stopped sharing any weight loss with her daughter or talking about clothing sizes until her little girl felt more comfortable about her body.

Judging others

We all judge the surrounding people. We live in a culture that consistently tells us we're not good enough, so our natural reaction is to look around at all the other humans dropping the ball.

When a friend announces her new life coaching business, you might think, "Don't you still live with your parents?" If someone tells us he's going to invest in a new startup, it opens up the opportunity to judge ourselves. "Gosh, I've never had enough in the bank to invest. He must have a lot more money than me."

These are ordinary, daily judgments, but they can build up and harm our well-being. Worse, if our kids hear us judging out loud, they see us as the people poised to judge them as well, and that can break down a relationship.

Did you ever hear that saying, "When you point at someone else, you point three fingers back at yourself?" My grandmother taught it to me one day in a mall when I was about six years old. I stood up to point at someone with an odd haircut, and my grandma grabbed my hand and showed how three fingers were indeed pointing at the judge, not the culprit.

A good friend of mine is a practicing Wiccan and told me this is one tenement of her religion.

"Everything you do comes back to you threefold," she said. "So it makes you pause and consider what you're putting into the world."

Okay, so judging others is a dangerous practice. But how do we catch ourselves in the act? And once caught, how do we stop?

First, we have to build our awareness. You can do this mentally, but I encourage you to grab a mini notebook or set of notecards and write any judgmental thoughts you have throughout the day.

See how many pages you fill. Once you have physical proof of your ongoing judgments, it becomes impossible to deny them.

Second, go through that list of judgments and adjust them into observational statements. For example:

Judgment - Cheryl never dresses appropriately for the office! She's always wearing old, ill-fitting suits that look like they need a trip to the cleaners.

Observation - Cheryl's clothes appear old and don't seem to fit her.

Stop there. Unless you get more information about why Cheryl dresses the way she does, you can't continue making mental value statements about her look.

After some practice writing out observations, make observational statements to your kids. "I see your plate still on the table, but dinner's over," or "It's 8 o'clock. That's bedtime."

Remember, kids don't judge. Naturally, they pick it up from the surrounding adults. A little two-year-old will say, "I broke my toy," where a four-year-old might decide, "I was clumsy and dropped my favorite toy!"

Whenever you hear a judgmental phrase from your child about him or herself, rephrase it. "Yes, you broke your toy. What can we do? Can we fix it? Do we need to look for a replacement?"

Whenever you hear a judgment about someone else, mention that you hear the judgment.

"Danny is so mean!"

"Oh, I hear a lot of judgment. Can you tell me what happened?" Get the focus on the facts, not the judgment itself. Whatever you do, don't validate it!

Finally, give yourself room to make mistakes. If you judge yourself or someone else, practice forgiveness. You're going to slip, and it's okay! The important thing is to make your way back to observational statements and a non-judgmental state of mind.

Living with anxiety

Now that you and your child are on the path to accepting anxiety, it's important to live with that anxious feeling.

To help kids better understand their anxiety, I often encourage them to think of it in a physical form and give it a name

One child, I'll call him Peter, and he calls his anxiety Ralph. Ralph is a tall, grey bunny with a sad face who lives in an old, dark house. Rather than waiting for

Ralph to take him by surprise, Peter draws Ralph pictures; he imagines visiting Ralph and sitting in his vegetable garden. Peter even saves a carrot or celery for Ralph once in a while and carries it outside where Ralph can find it.

Children don't have to manage their anxiety exactly like this. Still, I mention this story because it's a great example of building a relationship with a more challenging part of ourselves. If some aspect of our personality works against us, we need to face it and get to know it. There may be a good reason we can't stand to be around a certain group of people or why church makes you sweat. But you'll never find the key to the cause if you ignore the problem.

Ralph, the sad rabbit, eventually revealed to my young client that he existed as a safeguard - the little boy witnessed a violent incident at a young age and no longer felt safe in the world. However, that revelation took a few years, and even afterward, the boy's anxiety continued to hound him.

Your son or daughter must find his or her way to live with the anxiety that already lives deep in their minds. They need to pay attention to what triggers their intense fears or panic attack and what it means to have anxiety. It would be best if you put extra effort into exploring this as well, as your child may not verbalize how he or she feels right away.

Creating an anxiety character can help, but it's also tricky. Your child may keep switching what form his anxiety takes for a long time until the right face appears. Then, find the best way to interact with that character. A mental health professional can help you, and your child finds a vocabulary to facilitate conversations about anxiety to make it an easier process.

At home, keep up open conversations, non-judgmental statements, and healthy practices. Monitor triggers and discusses them in a positive, uplifting way whenever you can so you better understand what anxiety does to your child.

Anxiety as excuse

Please don't misunderstand my belief that anxiety must be a part of life. I do not want your child to go through life with a free pass simply because she is anxious.

In my career, I met several children whose parents immediately excused them from doing anything strenuous, unpleasant, or from taking responsibility simply because of an emotional issue. If one of these parents saw her son push your little boy - oh well, he has anxiety.

Make it clear to your child that anxiety is not an excuse; it's a situation. She needs to take on her anxiety and manage it, not let it impede living a full, rewarding life.

Imagine if your child simply hated cleaning. Rather than argue, you decide you'll wash the dishes, pick up his or her things, and make the bed. But then, your child grows up and eventually goes to a university several hours away from your house. Once he or she studies and deals with daily life on their own, suddenly everything is filthy. They have none of the skills to keep a dorm room clean, so soon they're living in squalor.

Learning to manage anxiety is like learning to clean up after ourselves. Dirt and disorganization are part of life. We can't avoid them and should never use them as an excuse to avoid something new and exciting. But, we have to clean our messes.

You'll have setbacks on the journey into maturity with an anxious child. Progress is never a straight path. It takes long detours and doubles back on itself all the time. The important thing you need to do is consistent.

"You have anxiety, and I want to help you manage your anxiety, but we'll never let this issue stop you from doing what you want to do. You're a beautiful person just the way you are."

4

ADDRESS LIMITING BELIEFS EARLY ON AND DEVELOP NEW BELIEF STRUCTURES

What are your beliefs?

I don't mean if you believe in God, humanity, or yourself. Rather, I mean, what shape do those beliefs take?

Let's use the church to start because it's a simple way to illustrate this issue. When you walk into a church, what do you expect? To hear horrifying descriptions of fire and brimstone, promise that you will burn for all eternity and that you are the worst of all sinners? Or, do you expect a warm, welcoming community where you can be yourself and find guidance?

Belief trips us up a lot. We have more than enough evidence that the church can terrify or soothe our souls. Yet, how we enter a religious organization changes everything about how we see it and interact with the people inside. If we expect non-stop judgment, we'll find it in neutral comments and casual looks. If we expect love and acceptance, we might miss a snide insult thrown our way.

The same happens with ourselves and our children. Our beliefs change the world. In the same way, what we believe about ourselves changes how we deal with problems, celebrate victories, and grow as people.

Our views on ourselves and how we interact with people can be broken down into two categories; interpersonal and intrapersonal.

Interpersonal beliefs change how we interact with others. Your interpersonal beliefs change how you interact with others. Do you expect the worst from those around you, or do you wait to see what they say and do before deciding if someone is a waste of time? When someone asks you about your day, do you talk for a moment and then ask them about their own, or do you talk non-stop until that person interrupts you?

The way we use our interpersonal beliefs can make us a joy or a chore to be around. Someone who constantly apologizes for everything may see herself as the source of all problems.

Ironically, that person then becomes an enormous problem, just not for the reason she thinks!

That kind of behavior is an example of a self-defeating interpersonal belief. But, the problem also goes the other way.

Have you ever met someone who constantly blames those around her for her own choices? That's a self-defeating interpersonal belief. Rather than focus on her actions and words, that individual looks outside herself for all the issues in her life.

That same person could internalize all that hurt and bewilderment and use it as proof that she'll never achieve the life she wants and never be perfect. That's a self-defeating intrapersonal belief.

When we blame ourselves for everything we do and for all the problems that go far beyond us, we do the same damage as those who constantly see themselves as victims.

Seeing the Truth

The reality of the situation is that anxiety takes our view and turns it into a kind of spotlight. We see what we want to in sharp, blinding detail, but everything beyond that falls into the dark. If it's not the thing making us anxious, we barely register its existence.

For example, you might be certain an upcoming performance will be a flop thanks to your inability to stop saying "Um..." Your heartbeat speeds up every time you practice, and you swear the word "Um" gets louder with each utterance.

You don't hear the rest of your speech, how fluidly you drop numbers and facts into the presentation, and how thoroughly you understand the material. Nope, your spotlight is on one word, so that's the only thing you can see.

A therapist friend of mine described one client's spotlight to me like a motorcycle driver who always turns left.

"He's so determined to see what's wrong, it takes his entire body to lean into the unpleasant side of things," she told me. "Once he started looking in the other direction, leaning to the right, he felt odd pains in his neck and shoulders. His dedication to worrying and stress was so deep it hurt to let it go."

How to turn the spotlight off

To redirect our beliefs, we have to change what we believe about our minds. Both kids and adults need to do this, and it takes a lot of practice, so I'll speak about everyone in this section.

To start, it's essential to reframe "thoughts" as "just thoughts." We do the same thing with a shortage of soda or a broken pencil.

"It's just soda. We'll buy more."

"Oh well, it's just a pencil."

Once we talk about our thoughts in the same way, "just a random thought, I'll have another," we stop giving so much control to our minds.

The human mind likes to worry. It prefers that we, its human shell that keeps it alive, stay safe. So, rather than ignore potential problems, it likes to mull them over for hours. But that worrying doesn't put us in actual danger. It only makes us think about something terrible that might happen.

Seeing as we can't stop worrying, we have to interact with worry in alternative ways. Try talking about this with your child in a context he can understand.

Compare worries to raindrops. You don't have to run and save one raindrop; there will always be more. Better to just let it fall on the house while you read a book and listen to the sound it makes.

Worries come and go like the rain - we can't stop it, but we can choose to focus on something we enjoy as we listen to it patter away.

If your child gravitates toward things that seem to reinforce his belief that the anxiety is the one he should listen to, not you, try to limit that resource. Social media might cause your child's belief that he is hated at school when in fact, only one or two bullies are the culprits.

Find the root of the problem and let your child know what you plan to do to solve it.

Limiting beliefs

One thing we all need to understand about ourselves is how our beliefs can limit our experiences. What are our limiting beliefs?

You hear people unintentionally limit themselves all the time. "I'm just not creative," they'll say, or, "I guess I'm just not a writer." At first, it feels like we're simply facing reality. I thought I could paint. I took a couple of classes, my paintings are, well, not great.

So, we label ourselves "not a painter" or "not creative." What's the harm?

The harm comes down the road. When we have time to do something else creative, maybe help design a logo at work or take part in an evening of wine and art, our brain gives us a little negative nudge.

"Hey, you already tried this, remember? It's better if you make some excuse and miss the event."

That's the problem with a mental label. Once there, it's challenging to get off. A friend of mine describes it as a "tattoo on the brain," and it feels that way.

Most of our limiting beliefs form in childhood, so you must discuss failed attempts in a way that doesn't build up those future walls, but allows for windows and doors.

If your child attempts to get a spot on the basketball team and doesn't get it, listen for how she talks about the experience.

"I suck at basketball," or "I should forget about sports," are comments that seem innocuous but can act as seeds for big, hard-to-pull-out weeds later on. Let's find another way to phrase these comments.

"I didn't do well at that last tryout. Maybe I can find someone on the team to work with me on my skills so I can make the next one."

"I love basketball, so I'm sad I'm not on the team. Maybe the school paper needs a sports reporter. I could go for the position, so I get to attend all the games."

The point is to turn this unpleasant experience into an opportunity. No one is so bad at basketball they should never pick up a ball again. Most of us can master basic skills, but only if we believe we can.

That's why limiting beliefs need to be reigned in. They shine the spotlight of negativity on what we don't have and make us miss all the other great things in our lives.

Limiting beliefs in early childhood

A child's earliest memories get seared into their brains. In the first six years of our lives, we soak up language more than anything, so comments made to us or about us can form us as people. It's easy to forget the power of words as adults; we've learned to let go of these things and move on, but the experience for little kids is quite different.

My father went through this at a young age. He learned about architects and how they designed buildings and loved the idea of doing that once he grew up. Unfortunately, he mentioned his dream to a thoughtless teacher who instantly dismissed the idea.

"You'll never be an architect," she told him. "You're not good at math."

That comment killed his dream on site. He went through life chasing other professions, but he never lost the sadness over that moment. One day he met a friend of mine who worked in architecture who assured him all the architects he knew hated math and struggled with it daily.

"Even me," she told him. "I'm the worst."

My dad's face fell. By then he was well into his fifties and had no intention of going back to school.

Knowing his teacher was mistaken made the experience worse. And now, it was too late to change his career.

Those brief comments can turn us inside out and change how we interact with the world. Think back to things people said about you when you were young, positive or negative.

Did any adult ever call you lazy, stupid? What about your peers in school? Were you bullied at a young age?

Those prior experiences can convince us we're not attractive, not talented, or worse, unloved. We only need to hear it once from someone in our lives; then, we'll repeat it to ourselves over and over.

Soon, the thing we believe is the truth.

That's why you must put your child in an environment where she hears comments about how loved, how important and beautiful she is as often as possible. If you see your child pulling away or become quieter than usual, investigate at school or daycare to see if there's a problem with another child or adult.

Many kids internalize the mean comments other children make and hang onto them for years. Talk to your child (or find a good children's book), about how to respond to mean comments and why some kids lash out. Focus on finding positive, uplifting friendships and help your child spend time with those children. Allow them to spend quality time together and then reflect on it with your son or daughter after the fact. Talk about how good it feels to have a great friend and how friendship strengthens us and makes us braver.

A quick word about kids in the minority: as your child goes to school, he or she may discover they're the only boy, girl, genderqueer student, Asian American, black student, etc. This puts a vast amount of pressure on students - no one likes to be in a place where no one else looks like them!

If this happens, advocate for your child. Meet with the teacher and say that you want him on the lookout for any racial or identity-based bullying, exclusion, or offhand comments. Offer to come and speak to the class about your background, bring snacks, etc., to help get the dialogue going in a positive direction.

The best time to do this is when your child is young, so don't miss this window. There's a slight chance you'll get another opportunity when your son or daughter is in high school, but don't count on it.

If you can get to those internalized statements early or help a mental health professional find your child's limiting beliefs, you can help tear them down. The sooner the better.

How to spot limiting beliefs

A great way to spot these harmful thoughts is through careful observation. Keep a small journal handy, or speak into your voice notes while you're out. See if you can find some of the following.

- Listen for toxic or harmful comments - Phrases like "I hate" or "I never" are the earmarks of a negative mindset. Pay attention when your child mentions he "hates" a class or a person and makes a note of it.

- Notice where your child feels challenged - What things come easily to your child, and where does he sigh in frustration? Those challenges may stem from an unspoken belief.

- Pay attention to what conflicts your child avoids - Can your son or daughter handle someone who takes their things or puts them down? If not, he or she may believe they're undeserving or unable to defend themselves.

Maintain your observations for a few weeks so you can spot patterns. Remember to keep your judgment in check as you practice observing. Don't let your bias blind you to the actual issue at hand.

Once you have some solid data, you can tackle the problem.

Limiting beliefs and anxiety

Why is all of this so important?

Unfortunately, these limiting beliefs apply directly to our thoughts about anxiety. Many patients tell me they need to worry. If they didn't worry, who knows what they might do.

What I find is that most people confuse worrying with preparation. They misuse the word. Instead of finding ways to "prepare" to leave a job, my client will "worry" about the consequences of leaving a job. Imagine if all that energy could be spent on looking at potential prospects, reaching out to his or her network, and finding out what other opportunities are right around the corner.

Of course, millions of people believe their anxiety keeps them safe. Anxiety can be a drag, sure, but without it, I might jump off a roof! Because so many people feel their negative or stressed-out mindset is the more grown-up version of themselves, they see no reason to leave it behind.

The worst belief I encounter is also the most prevalent. That's the belief that worrying is another kind of motivation.

This is tricky because yes, worrying can spur you to action. If you're worried the building you're standing in is about to collapse; you'll run out the door. But, there's no guarantee you won't run right into a blazing fire or towards a dangerous person.

Worrying often leads to rushed decisions or choices made without clear thought. When we value our worrying mind, we stop listening to our inspiration or our joy. We settle for a life we can have instead of reaching for one we want.

It's hard to see how much we limit ourselves with our beliefs about anxiety until we step away from those beliefs. And that takes work.

How to overcome limiting beliefs

Don't put this off! It's essential to get positive, open-minded beliefs for your child to improve their anxiety and stress management to help them feel empowered and able to take on anything. As soon as you have a good handle on what mental limits your child may hold onto, you can start.

First, get your environment sorted out. If your house has a lot of clutter or extra stuff, it's time to go through and minimize it. Use the Marie Kondo system if you like - start by going through your clothing, books, papers, miscellaneous things like stored items or old toys, and finally, anything sentimental.

Get your entire family in on the process. Talk about why you're keeping some things and getting rid of the rest, why you want your home to be an orderly and friendly place. Then cover who gets your old stuff via donations or a yard sale. Let them know they're helping someone else with their old toys or baby clothes.

If you simply don't have time to keep house, consider giving other members of your family different chores with a simple reward system. The internet modem comes out once everyone's tasks are done, for example.

Second, try a minimalist approach (or an approximation of it), in your home. Minimalism is a new attitude about shopping for everyday things like clothing or pantry staples. Rather than trying to fill your closet or pack in the snacks, live on the bare minimum.

A minimalist closet comprises ten complete outfits, nothing extra. A minimalist pantry has one snack per family member. It's a big switch for most people, but many find the minimalist approach to be an immense relief.

When we surround ourselves with stuff, we get overwhelmed, or we forget what we already have.

We can barely see half of it!

Don't jump into minimalism all at once. Start with one aspect of your life (like your shoe rack) and see how it goes. Make sure your child sees you doing it first, and talk about how it makes you feel to get down to the essentials. After a period of modeling, ask (don't demand), if your son might want to try getting down to the basics in a craft corner or with clothing.

Third, try experimenting with your comfort zone. This is another activity for the entire family. Get everyone together and make a list of things most or none of you have done before. Have you rafted down a river? Eaten Ethiopian food? Tried to communicate in Sign Language?

Then choose one thing per month for the entire family to try. Use this opportunity to communicate why you're doing this and how it can help you. Limiting your actions leads to a closed mind, so trying new things can help you see the world differently and therefore, yourself.

Finally, if possible, go for a round of counseling. Every family benefits from a round of counseling, so schedule yours for a whole-group session. Remember, going to counseling or therapy doesn't mean your family has anything wrong with it. Your session is a chance to get to know one another in an alternative way and open the lines of communication.

Building up new beliefs

Once you break down old, harmful thought patterns, help your child build up good ones to take their place. Luckily, this is a much more straightforward process.

Here are some everyday things you can do to steer them towards positive, uplifting thoughts.

- Praise them - Make sure your praise for your child truly reflects what you see in her actions. If your child loves to draw, don't focus on technique but on the fact you love to see her creativity. "You're so creative! I love to see it," is a great comment. If you notice her reading a book to a younger sibling or deep in thought, mention how much you love their kindness or ability to reflect.

- Offer freedom with friends - This one needs to be within limits, of course, but give as much space to your child and a friend as you can. Avoid supervising to where you interrupt

their game or session of pretend. If your child
gets upset by something a friend says or does,
he will tell you. If no one's crying, take a seat
and relax.

- Show you trust them - A lot of children feel
supervised to the point of exhaustion. You
must show your child that they have your
trust as long as they don't betray it. Give your
child one reminder to do a chore, then say
nothing about it again until bedtime. If the
task gets done, great! Offer some praise. If it
doesn't, simply state, "Hey, you didn't clean
up your stuff in the bathroom like I asked, so
no video games tomorrow." Keep emotion out
of the equation - focus on what you want and
what happens if you don't get it.

- Set goals - Goal setting can help kids
immensely and get the phrase "I can't" out of
their vocabulary. Start small and use things
they already do. If your child loves to play
catch, set the goal of catching a ball from
further away. Then find time to practice each
day and work on moving further and further
apart until he or she reaches that new limit.
Celebrate once you get there! These little
practices make larger, long-term goals feel less

intimidating and make kids ask, "What can I do to get to my goal?"

- Set reasonable boundaries - Whatever your child is into, make sure your rules about it reflect their age and maturity level. For example, if your child wants an Instagram account at nine, simply say no. Social media before the age of 13 is highly discouraged for its negative effect on brain development. Tell your child, "The answer is no. When you're 13, we'll get you a private account." It's not a debate. You're the parent, and you get to decide. Again, keep emotion out of it. You're simply setting a boundary, and that's your role in a child's life.

- Also, make sure you don't make everything perfect all the time. It's okay if a family portrait doesn't turn out the way you dreamed or if all your efforts to minimize the stuff in your house and keep it clean blow up in your face. That's life sometimes.

- Make sure your kids see you handle mistakes in a calm, realistic way and then ask for their help in finding a solution. If you model reaching out for help, they'll do it, too.

Raise empowered kids

A great way to combat limited mindsets is to help kids feel empowered. We can do this in lots of small ways throughout the day. Here's a quick look at some simple ways to empower your child every day.

- Offer choice - Young kids need this in limited quantities (only three), but older kids can work with whatever's available. Show your younger child three bowls of cereal and ask, "Which one would you like today?" and then serve his choice. Older kids love to choose their clothing, so walk into a clothing store and give your kid a budget. Again, this needs to have some limits (nothing inappropriate for school, for example), but trust that he can choose his outfits.

- Talk about body safety - A kid who grows up with an understanding of things like grooming or a predator's reliance on secrets is far less likely to fall victim. Body safety education also helps kids understand that they have agency over themselves. No one should ever make them feel obligated to let them play with their hair, for example. If someone makes them uncomfortable, they need to pay attention and talk to you about it. There are some influential books available that help young readers understand the issue. Older kids need literature, too, so keep books about body biology, sex education, and gender issues available at home.

- Manage risk - Let your child try something without constant safety concerns. Climbing trees, playing in the rain, speeding down the street on a bike might cause an injury, but kids learn from injuries! Remember, everything might go incredibly well. Your child may have the best day of his life.

- Make room for interests - Even if your child's interest completely mystifies you, let her explore it. Remember, the job market is packed with positions that didn't exist back when you were in school. The thing your child loves might lead to a unique opportunity. Even if your kid obsesses over Japanese foxes, be supportive.

- Encourage perseverance - Talk to your kids about what to do when things get complicated. Share stories about hard things you've had to do in life or at work and what happened when you quit or kept going. When you see your child getting ready to quit, see what you can do to help him finish. Or, find someone else who might have some insight into the situation and can support your son.

We'll talk more about healthy habits and how to keep kids empowered in chapter five.

5

HEALTHY ALTERNATIVES

Now that you have a better idea of what's happening in your child's brain and why it's time to put some healthy practices in place. Most of the work happens through open, neutral communication. But hey, we all slip, and that's okay!

So, what are some ways we can keep the conversation about emotions and our feelings about our feelings open? Of course, it takes time, but you can start with some basics in conversation with your son or daughter.

Talking to kids

You're a parent, so I know I don't have to tell you that deep, meaningful conversations with children of any age can be a real feat. I know when my son attended preschool I wanted every detail of his day, but all I got was a grunt of "School's good."

The problem is that most kids are still developing the mindset or high order thinking; it takes time to dive into the details of a conversation. That's where you come in. As a parent, you can help him, or her develop that skill with daily practice.

Preschoolers

Preschoolers learn and develop at light speed, but they don't know how to recount their day, certainly not to an adult. That an adult doesn't know everything he does during school might seem odd to someone whose life is so closely monitored. That's why you need to phrase questions in a way he or she can understand.

Try to avoid open-ended questions like, "How was school?" To a young child, this is not an invitation to a great, detailed answer. Instead, it's an invitation to say school was good or bad, fun or boring, etc. Open questions work well with older, more mature people, but kids need more direction.

Instead, try checking the day's schedule and asking, "What did you make with the teacher after lunch today?" or "Did you play with Samuel?" Those specific, closed questions help kids talk about what happened and how they felt about it.

If you notice a shift in your child's emotions, try asking about something observable, like an expression on her face, or an unusual amount of silence.

Try asking, "Did I see you with a sad face when I picked you up from school today? Did something happen?" It's hard to deny what others can see, so this is an excellent way to check in on your child emotionally.

A quick note about responding: first, don't interrupt. Remember, a brief silence is okay. Also, keep your face neutral as you listen. Young children pick up on every facial tick, so remember to keep yours serene, so you don't cause any undue stress. If you feel like there's something you need to learn more about, like a bully or a problem at school, contact the classroom's teacher or the school administration.

Elementary kids

Young children spend their school days in a high-energy environment that can be non-stop. One minute they're practicing spelling, then suddenly they're off to the gym, then they spin around and run to the computer lab for a digital project. It's a lot.

That's why I encourage parents to save questions about the child's day for after dinner or during a long drive home. If you bombard your daughter with 20 questions, the moment you pick her up outside the classroom, it can be too much. Kids need their transition out of the classroom to be a peaceful moment so they can wind down.

Instead of asking lots of questions to your child, use that pickup moment to offer to carry things like a jacket or a backpack. Show your daughter that you're there for them and ready when they are for a long talk.

Save the evenings for a parent-kid moment, like putting together a puzzle or coloring a picture. That way, you make yourself available for her with no pressure. If you want your child to open up about her day, start by sharing details about your day.

Remember to listen with an open mind and not interrupt. Set your phone aside and have it on silent during this quality time. Keep reinforcing that you, the parent, are available for your kid, not a judge waiting to hammer your gavel. That will make you the first person your child goes to when he or she has a problem in the future.

Tweens

Kids between 10 and 13 are likely going through puberty and feeling incredibly uncomfortable in their bodies. That makes deep and vulnerable conversations feel like torture as kids in this stage are on high alert that everyone around them can see their shortcomings.

This makes communication shut down for a lot of families. Parents want to communicate, but conversations either end in tears or slammed doors. Everyone's feeling too sensitive or too exposed.

The car can be a good problem solver. No one's making eye contact, so it's easier to talk to one another and open up. Listen actively, don't take any phone calls, and reinforce details of the story with minor questions like, "What did you say after Sammy said that to you?"

Be careful not to fix everything. Many parents want to direct their children's social lives, but I encourage you to let your child make mistakes and reflect on them. I know a lot of parents who try to pick their child's friends, but this is almost guaranteed to backfire. It's impossible to see how a friendship will play out. Take a back seat and remind yourself that the only way your child can have meaningful connections in his life is if he is authentic, not scripted.

With tweens, it's also important to schedule a kid-parent date with your son or daughter. This can be as simple as watching a TV show together on a Saturday afternoon. Don't make it all about talking or reflecting. Instead, use this opportunity to pay attention to what your child likes, what they're growing out of, and why.

As always, withhold judgment. This can be tough! Media designed for young children often feels aggravating to adults, but that's normal. Unfortunately, your brain doesn't function like a child's anymore, so you need to take a deep breath and sit through the incredibly repetitive music or painfully slow manga. Your efforts will pay off, I promise!

Teenagers

My favorite group, teenagers, offers unique challenges to parents at all times. It's incredible to me how every parent seems to believe that, sure, teens can be difficult, but *my child* will be fine.

I have news for you - your child will more than likely be a self-centered, rude, thoughtless teenager. It's no one's fault; it's a crucial phase in brain development. From 14 to 19, the brain only cares about social interactions and meaningful connections. Unfortunately, it's also got a much bigger pleasure center, so it's hard for teenagers to understand why a thrilling jump from the roof to a trampoline is a bad idea - the logical brain is not in control right now.

So, how do we talk to someone who isn't interested in anything parents have to say or who can't think through a situation logically? There are a few ways, but you have to adjust to less conversation.

First, set clear boundaries with friends and any romantic interests. State clearly what your rules are for curfew, how many people can be in the house, what areas they can use, when your permission is required, etc. Then lay out consequences and stick to them.

A friend of mine limits tech time for her family by keeping chargers in a secret spot. Everyone gets two charges a week, so they have to manage their device accordingly. If someone needs the internet for school, they can use her computer in plain view of the rest of the family. That's it.

It sounds harsh, but those rules keep everyone from staring down at their phones all day. Her family gets in the occasional conversation. It's outstanding.

The other thing you need to do, and stay firm on this, is family mealtimes. Look at your schedule and find at least a few days a week you and your entire family can sit down to the same meal. Don't allow for interruptions, and model the conversation you hope to see. Remember, teenagers are constantly hungry, so use that to your advantage.

When you ask questions, try staying curious. Start questions with "What do you think" or "I wonder." Try to avoid the phrase "Why did you..." when you want to know something. "Why did you choose that outfit?" is an example of a question a teen will read as judgmental, even if you didn't mean it that way.

Finally, communicate through text messages or video chats. Find the medium that helps your child open up and try doing it that way. You might surprise yourself and find your love talking over an app or showing emotion with silly images. Teenagers have a lot to show us. We just have to pay attention and stay open.

But what about helping your kids express themselves?

Teaching healthy expression

As your child grows up, you can model good listening and how to stay calm in emotional situations. Here are a few basic things you can do to help your child understand good ways to express him or herself.

When your child is very young, respond when she calls out to you. This shows your child that you're listening and available for them. I've met some parents who disagree with me on this one, but I consistently talk to young clients who feel secure in their belief that their parents "never listen."

Remember, the listening habits you establish with your child in those early years will stick with you as they grow older. So if you want them to listen, listen first.

Then you need to know when something is a genuine reaction, like real fear or frustration, and when it's part of a phase, like a tantrum. Anytime your child throws himself onto the floor to kick and scream about a toy, you can laugh it off. Tantrums are more about testing limits than anything else.

However, if your child freezes or looks distraught, take him aside and ask how he is feeling. Your child's eyes will tell you when something is wrong more than anything else. Pay attention to the shifts in your child's face to know when you need to intervene and when it may not be such a big deal.

Another significant thing to practice is the "I" statement. This puts your words in a different context and removes the judgment.

You can try them by adjusting statements like this:

"You're being so rude right now!" becomes "I feel hurt when you slam the door like that. I don't want us to treat each other that way."

They take practice, but a mental professional can help. Rephrasing common statements so they focus on you directly and your experience helps your kids build up empathy for you and feel closer to you. It also models good communication.

Helping kids take charge

How can we show kids their incredible potential? Through small opportunities to be in charge of something, they can manage.

Helping kids take charge of different aspects of their lives can be a journey. Everyone responds to different things, so be aware that your efforts may need to adjust as you go. Take the time to discuss with your partner the different things your child may be ready to handle.

An excellent place to start is their bedrooms. See if your son might be interested in painting the walls a different color or changing some decoration. Ask if there's a character or person they like that might make for a fun poster.

Try to give your child the most personalized space you can to help them feel like their interests and hobbies matter. If you have a child who loves to dance, see if you can create a space in the garage or somewhere in the house for them to practice. If your child lives for working with his hands, find some smaller tools or a safe way to help him create at home.

Another great way to empower your child safely and respectfully is to encourage them to find a quiet space outside. You may be lucky enough to live somewhere near a lake, beach, or forest, which is perfect. If not, the nearest park or a spot on the roof can work. The important thing is to let your child choose this space on their own.

When kids have a place, they can call their own and sit with themselves for long periods, they become more self-aware, have an easier time managing emotions, and feel trusted by their parents.

As they get older, they won't struggle to calm down in stressful situations, they'll know the power of stepping aside when things get heated, and they'll have an easier time reflecting and taking in what's happening, not the "what ifs" in their mind.

Helping kids set goals

We rarely see kids setting and achieving goals, but that's usually because they don't have the same vocabulary as the surrounding adults. Does your child have a dream? Absolutely! But she may only express them a certain way.

A great way to look at this is with what's known as the growth mindset. The growth mindset means we understand no one is set in stone - everyone can change. All it takes is a set of goals and the right mentality to achieve them.

To help younger kids understand goals and the process to achieve them, here's a quick exercise to help your child visualize it all together.

Ask the right questions

Sit down with your daughter and a nice little journal. Ask the following questions to get the conversation started.

"Hey, I want to help you set a goal. So tell me, what's something you wish you could do?" Or, "What would you do if you had no fear and knew you would do it perfectly the first time?"

Their answers might surprise you. It might be, "Jump over the house," or "Be invisible." Write whatever they say. You can always add something more realistic later.

Look at their answers and ask follow-up questions like, "How would that improve your life?" or "Would that help your friends or your family?" These aren't judgments; they're investigations into why your child wants to leap over houses. Maybe she wishes dearly to be an athlete or have some space from the surrounding people.

Then make the goal a plan. Break down the goal "be more athletic" into small goals. Draw a ladder or staircase to hold the plan to show how one achievement leads to the next. See if you can get the more broad ideas into something specific (I want to be a baseball player, for example). Then break down what's already available to your child, what items you have in the house or can get cheap or for free.

Now you can look at habit changes. What skills do baseball players need to practice? How often? Who can practice with you? Start with a small goal -

I will play catch every day after school

- and acknowledge when your child sticks to it. If she ditches the dream, it may result from an obstacle. She may feel too tired after school to do something physical; she might realize she picked a sport she doesn't care for or feel frustrated with a lack of progress.

Before you let her give up, do some reflecting and brainstorm potential solutions. Then talk about what other obstacles may arise. She might need to do some other activity that interrupts practice time. She might get sick and need a break. Acknowledge that every goal means work and perseverance, but a positive attitude can get us to the finish line.

Setting healthy expectations

We all set expectations for ourselves, particularly with our goals, but it rarely takes long before getting a reality check. It's essential to manage our expectations and be realistic long before we work towards a goal.

For kids, this often involves brainstorming. Start with what your child assumes he should achieve in life. Does he believe it's important to be famous, popular, or well-liked? What about the goal of fitting in? Does he want to be considered a leader, or blend in so completely no one pays any attention?

Talk about your child's existing expectations and some dangers of things like fame, wealth, or popularity. These things often lead to emptiness, not happiness or a contented sense of well-being. Like a slim waistline or youthful beauty, even things presented as important can be more fabrication than reality.

Look at some videos online exposing how models look in real life as opposed to their photos. Ask your child, "Why would someone want everyone to think they look different from what they really appear?" These themes seem lofty, but it's been my experience that we can understand the overwhelming desire to be loved from an incredibly young age.

After you break down some downfalls of these superficial goals, let your child know what you expect as a parent. Do you expect your child to be respectful, clean, happy? Let him know. Mention nothing like weight or grades. If your child already feels anxious over these things, hearing you insist on these goals can make it much worse. Wait until you see your child make some progress towards a less stressful life before you approach those subjects.

When you want to nail down more specific expectations, think about how you can take an aspiration like,

"I want my child to be a good student," and think about what that means.

An outstanding student isn't necessarily a child with a perfect set of grades. Teachers rarely get excited about someone who can come in and ace every test. Instead, they gush about kids who love to learn, who ask questions, and who love to follow up on a class independently with a good book or an online investigation.

So, you can adjust your "good student" expectation into "I want my child to enjoy learning in and out of school."

Here are a few more examples of how to keep expectations healthy and positive:

I want my child to have a healthy physique — I want my child to have a good relationship with food and enjoy some kind of sport or outdoor activity.

I want my child to attend a good university — I want to help my child find a school that best fits his or her needs and career goals.

I want my kid to have a good job — I want to make sure my son or daughter understands what kind of career he or she wants and what steps can make that job a reality.

I want my kid to fit in -- I hope my child finds great friends that he or she can have as a support system for years to come.

Don't insist your child fit one mold or another. We often think we know what path our child should take, but it's rare we find the right one even with the best of efforts. I've met hundreds of parents who wring their hands over the fact their child chose a different profession after years of medical school or worry their child isn't making enough money. I always ask them to consider how their child feels about her choices. Are they happy? Do they have wonderful friendships? Do they go to bed hating their life, or do they love how they live?

Those are the questions I wish more parents would ask.

Creating good habits

When kids are young, they want specific things. Sweet foods, insanely stimulating media, repetition, these things collide into a childhood. As parents, we know our kids need healthy meals and relaxing moments, but it's tough to provide them when our children insist on precisely the opposite.

You can make some changes without involving your kids (though you might want to) to help them feel better and grow up with significantly less anxiety. Luckily, we live in a time when healthy alternatives for everything from baking to breakfast cereals are quickly taking up real estate on supermarket shelves.

Sugar

We all love sugar. I grew up with two incredible grandmothers who stuffed me full of homemade pies and chocolate pudding until I came to expect them at every meal. My father baked cakes constantly and my mom baked cookies weekly. When I got older and started packing on weight, I knew sugar was the culprit, but I did not know how to cut it out of my diet.

Once I started reading more about how sugar affects a young child's brain, I looked back on those dessert binges with alarm. Sugar is not something a kid's brain needs, no matter how much they want it.

Sugar interacts with neurotransmitters of the brain and affects dopamine levels, which is why we associate sweet foods with happiness. Packaged treats have vast amounts of chemical food dyes (more on that later), to make them nice and colorful, another thing meant to make kids insist you buy them.

Unfortunately, kids who consume foods high in sugar regularly are more likely to have sleep issues, a more challenging time controlling their actions and emotions, and struggle to pay attention. Yes, they love them, but those brightly colored candies can keep your child from learning, getting a good night's sleep, or struggling to express themselves.

What to do? Take stock of the pantry with your partner or the entire family and look for anything with high amounts of added sugar. Start with the obvious things like sweet cereals or sauces, cookies, and other sweets. Also, check your drinks. Many juices come with high amounts of added sugar even though the packaging insists the beverage is healthy or natural.

Get rid of anything causing the sugar rush. I know this is tough and often, this means throwing out or giving away something you never had time to open. I promise it's worth it.

Then, the next time you go shopping, look for some of these alternatives:

Instead of... Buy...

- candy or packaged sweets buy in-season fruits from a local grower

- a bag of white sugar buy monk fruit sweetener, date sugar, or coconut sugar

- soda buy fizzy water to mix with freshly squeezed juice

- chocolate or strawberry milk buy fresh fruit or cacao nibs to blend with milk at home

- creamy, sugary popsicle buy natural fruit popsicles (or molds to make your own frozen treats)

I know this list won't be ideal for everyone, but you get a general idea. Many brands hear the outcry for less or no sugar in their foods and answer with innovative products. It's now possible to buy sugar-free cereals and grain-free snacks from lots of brands. It means looking a little harder in the grocery store and possibly frequenting farmer's markets, but with some hunting, you can find a lot of great stuff.

This is also an excellent opportunity to do some growing at home if you have space. Even a few pots on a windowsill can make something like carrots or tomatoes a lot more exciting. If you're lucky enough to have access to a fruit orchard or a local farm that can let your kids take a tour, sign the family up for a visit. Seeing where real, healthy food comes from helps children feel more connected to what they eat.

Lactose

One of the most problematic foods for our bodies to break down is ironically also one of the most popular. Dairy in all its forms can cause many reactions, from skin rashes to diarrhea, in kids and adults.

I grew up in a rural area where enormous glasses of milk were a part of every meal. My parents also believed firmly that my brothers and I would grow up with brittle bones and poor health without dairy in our lives.

Now I am lactose intolerant to where I barely look at the dairy section. To my shock, diary was unnecessary to keep up my calcium (it turns out it's in almost every fruit and vegetable), and there are plenty of alternatives.

I was even more shocked to read about the connection between dairy and behavioral issues. The protein casein, which is the main ingredient in cheese, appears to be linked to impulsivity and hyperactivity. Kids on diets without dairy seem to manage their emotions much more easily than those who are quick to eat lots of cheese, cream, or milk.

There are several theories why this happens, but casein has a simple effect on our bodies. Either we have an allergic reaction to it (or lactose intolerance), or it can ping our pleasure center so hard we roll our eyes in ecstasy. Either way, this is a reaction that should have us concerned.

Try some non-dairy recipes at home. I often hunt for vegan, Asian, or Paleo recipes as these never include cheese in the ingredient list. Or, if you worry you won't be able to live without cheese in your life, look for one of the many vegetable-based products available now. Vegan cheeses are getting so good they're winning awards at food shows. Take advantage and try one out with your kids.

Artificial Food Dyes

The packaged food industry brought food dyes into our diets. These colorful additives can seem innocuous - it's just color, after all. What's the harm?

It turns out. The UK banned several food dyes from consumer products after a study of dyed drinks showed how artificial colors could affect a child's mood and hyperactivity. The Food Standards Agency used the results as proof that parents needed to keep artificially dyed foods away from their kids.

Sadly, these dyed goodies are aimed directly at the people who shouldn't eat them - our darling children. An excellent way to avoid temptation is to first make safe, naturally dyed foods at home. Look for dyes made from fruits and vegetables in the store if you'd like to keep making colorful treats. Things like powdered beetroot or acai can help bring that extra pizzazz to your home cooking.

Consider having your groceries delivered or ready for pick up to avoid the impulse buy section with all the chocolates and candies by the cash register. If that's not an option, stick to the edges of the grocery store when you have children with you. That will help you avoid walking by the snacks or colorful treats so they won't be at the forefront of your child's mind while they're in the store. If your kids don't see them, they're less likely to want them.

Caffeine

Finally, caffeine. This chemical affects everyone differently, so experiment with this one to see if it hurts or helps.

Don't give caffeine to any child under the age of 15, and then use it sparingly. If you have a caffeine-loving teenager in your home, pay attention to how much your son or daughter drinks and look for alternatives. Green and black tea also have significant amounts of caffeine, but herbal tea has zero and can be bought in the same shops or stores as coffee.

If you notice your child struggles to get to sleep, stay focused, or often has severe headaches, caffeine may be the issue. Talk to them about taking a break from sodas or coffee to see if he or she feels better, but warn them that there will be a couple of days of withdrawal. Have some headache meds on hand (make sure they don't also have caffeine), and brace yourself.

It may help if you take a break from caffeine and show solidarity. Many of my clients found that a vacation from caffeine made them a lot more productive, gave them a better night's sleep, and cut down their stress. Best of all, they could indulge in a cup or two on intense days for a tremendous jolt of energy, then go back to their caffeine-free existence.

Other healthy habits

Once you have the food situation handled, remember to keep learning and to go easy on yourself. You may have days when you break down and buy everyone triple-chocolate ice cream and espresso shots, but that doesn't mean you're doing anything wrong. You're human and you can't hold yourself to impossible standards. Remember to do what works for you and be gentle with yourself.

To help build up a suitable set of habits and a solid base of strength, both physical and mental, I encourage you and your family to exercise every day.

Why exercise? First, it's free mental health. I don't particularly care how much you weigh; you should work out to help balance the chemicals in your mind and allow yourself to let go of the stress of the day. Daily exercise can be as or more effective than medication for depression and anxiety. It helps you see how strong and dependable you are with each movement.

Second, exercise decreases muscle tension, literally taking the stress out of your body. We all store stress in one section of our body or another, and that causes long-term damage. Get your muscles moving so they don't tear, swell, or stiffen up.

Third, exercise directly benefits your heart. When you work out, you give your heart a tremendous benefit. The increase in heart rate helps your brain release endocannabinoids, your body's natural drug for that nice high after a workout.

Exercising as a family

If you're lucky enough to get together and do something physical as a group, get your family to go outside and play tag, ride bikes, roller skate, anything that keeps everyone moving. Keep your watch on to make sure the game or the outing lasts a minimum of sixty minutes. If your children are still very small (between 2 and 5), they may want to go for much longer! You can sit and watch after an hour, but your children need to see their parents exercising. That way, they'll understand it as a lifelong habit, not just something for kids.

As your kids get older, try signing up for an online dance studio or find some free videos of yoga classes,

HIIT workouts, or find a trainer who can work with everyone together. Talk to your family about what everyone likes to do and try out a few different styles of exercise to see what clicks.

Another great way to do this is to challenge one another to be the workout leader. Put your five-year-old in front of everyone and have him or her lead some movements for a song, then switch. If you have teenagers who love to run or play a sport, ask them to teach the family some skills to share their passion.

Working out individually

I completely understand that you and your family may not get together for a group workout, at least not regularly. Don't stress; focus on celebrating everyone's progress together in their physical pursuits.

First, make sure everyone has access to some kind of physical activity they enjoy, yourself included. If all you have time to do is roll out your yoga mat for an early morning session, guard that time. It's important! Let your family know that you are not available for any parent duties once you're on your mat. Once you get out of the shower dressed and prepared for the day, they can come to you with questions or help.

As for your kids, talk to their school about what clubs, sports, or activities are available and get a good idea of what's possible for you and your child. Talk to your son or daughter about what speaks to him or her. If your child insists on video games, say they have to get some kind of system that involves moving around, not sitting and staring for hours and hours.

Then, encourage everyone to talk about what's happening in their sport or activity. If there's an exhibition or big game, make sure everyone attends and cheers for the family member in the competition. And circle back to healthy expectations. Use the upcoming Tae Kwon Do exhibit as an opportunity to set a goal.

I want to earn a better score than the last exhibit.

I want to earn my next belt before the month is over.

And so on. Let your kids hear you set goals for yourself too. If you live for yoga, give yourself the goal of a tricky balance pose or handstand, then talk about what you have to do to achieve it. Be open about your process, and be sure to share your victories as you go.

If you make a mistake, talk about it. Encourage your kids to discuss what's making them frustrated, how they want to improve, and what it means to get more agility, faster speed, anything they might aim for.

Keep listening and sharing. That's the best thing any parent can do.

. . .

Yoga and meditation

I want to take a moment to add some notes on yoga and meditation. I love both because they're an easy addition to any exercise routine. A quick video search will show you things like Yoga for Runners, Yoga for Hockey, and a vast amount of other options. Meditation is also a great habit to instill in your daily routine as well as your children's.

Yoga only requires a mat or soft carpet. Many companies want to convince you to buy special outfits, towels, and props, but the truth is none of it is necessary for a good session. Yoga is available to any age or ability level and has endless benefits for anyone who gives it a chance.

For anyone working, going to school, or simply growing, yoga helps build flexibility, endurance, strength, and well-being. Please don't feel that you can't do it because you're not flexible enough. Yoga will help that flexibility come later.

The most critical element of this style of exercise is the focus on breathing. The word yoga means connection, as in a relationship between moving and breathing. A lot of yoga sessions begin with the teacher taking a moment and getting everyone to breathe together. This mental break helps us clear our minds and get our stress and anxiety down significantly.

Yoga for kids is often a lighter, sillier approach, with children acting out different characters like a clock or a bouncy spring. Children's yoga doesn't focus on breathing because breath control can challenge kids in a way that frustrates rather than calms them down. However, there is a period at the end that helps them lie back, close their eyes, and imagine nice things - something all of us need!

No matter what sport your kids enjoy, encourage them to add yoga to their regimen. It can help prevent injuries and improve their focus, but it also keeps emotions under control. Yoga builds a calm state of mind with static poses. It helps us pay attention to how we feel physically, which builds our awareness of how we feel mentally.

The meditation that comes at the end of the class feels so natural that participants often slip into a solid five minutes of mental calm with no effort at all. That meditation can include anything from listening to chimes to picturing a floating cloud.

Meditation and the habit of meditating have lifelong benefits. The most obvious is a reduction in stress and impulsive behavior. Longer, fewer surface benefits include better decision-making, enhanced memory in the short and long term, and deeper concentration. It also helps us sleep, builds up strength in our immune system, and allows us to experience a deeper, more satisfying level of happiness.

Do your best to create a space where your kids can meditate for a few minutes a day. Let them see you and your partner do it as well to reinforce the importance of the practice. For kids with anxiety, this skill is invaluable.

MODEL BEHAVIOR

In the pages of this book, I covered lots of different ways to improve your child's relationship with her anxiety, but these can sometimes feel like quick fixes or things that may fade away after a few weeks.

How can we take everything we discussed in this book and turn it from a temporary solution to a lifelong habit for your child?

The best way is to model what you want to see in your child.

Think of it this way. I know a lot of parents who yell things at their children. They insist, loudly, that their son or daughter "FOCUS!" or "BE QUIET!" It often feels like kids aren't listening to us unless we're yelling, but I can guarantee you that if you shout, soon you'll have a house filled with screaming kids. Not because you told them to shriek at the top of their lungs, but because that's the action they see when you try to get what you want.

I often encourage parents to think about what adults they want their children to be, then to act like that kind of adult. I remind them to know constantly that their sons and daughters soak in every detail of what their parents say and do. Do you come home complaining, griping about your terrible job and the idiots with whom you interact every day? Then prepare for your kids to do the same.

None of this is to make you feel like an inadequate parent or to say that I blame moms and dads for every emotion their child feels. That isn't fair and makes no sense. An anxious child doesn't need someone to blame for his emotions. What they need is to be in a place where it's okay to talk about how we feel, to go to therapy, to be upset, even if it's seemingly over nothing.

Homes that foster an open mind about feelings, self-improvement, and intrapersonal knowledge are places where kids can work through their anxiety. Of course, they still feel it, sometimes to the point of a full panic attack, but they don't attach any negativity or shame to their anxiousness. Instead, they work to understand it because that's what their parents do.

. . .

Children are copycats

Your child's home is her first classroom. Children learn through listening to those around them, copying the words they hear or actions they see, and then taking in the consequences. Maybe they get ignored; perhaps the phrase earns her a punishment. No matter the outcome, that becomes a lesson for your child.

What can parents do? How do we make this a positive experience in a child's life yet still teach them right from wrong?

There are several ways to manage your own emotions and make sure your child knows what you want and do not want them to do. First, however, it's essential to check your reactions foremost.

Show Them

Humans are social beings, so we learn how to act in the world through Social Learning Theory. We don't read about how to be human; we observe others around us and gradually take on their language, gestures, and behaviors.

For example, if every adult moved around the house by crawling, all babies would forgo walking and continue crawling for years. But, because they see adults standing up, they want to stand. That's why baby's first steps feel so exciting - our tiny children are gradually becoming adults.

The same thing happens with emotional expression. For example, there's a brilliant film about adoption and how the foster care system can shape children called Instant Family. In it, there's a scene in which a small girl sits her doll at a table and immediately berates it.

"You better not embarrass me at this restaurant!" she yells, her face twisted up into a classic angry mom's expression.

The girl turns to the woman playing pretend with her and adds, "Don't you tell me how to raise my daughter!"

It's played for both laughs and shock value. The anger sounds hilarious coming from a six-year-old in her backyard, but it also makes us realize that she's acting out something that happened to her. She's taking on the role of the mother that yelled at her as a small child.

Any teacher can tell you whose parents curse or openly discuss unsavory topics at home because the children of those parents come to school and repeat it. Many parents assume a child who plays quietly at home does so everywhere, but I can attest that most kids let a different side of their personality show once the parents aren't around. Those soft-spoken kids hold court on the playground; the confident, smiley kid sulks all day; the little boy who insists he doesn't like books hides in the library at recess.

These switches happen because kids can tune into exactly what parents want and how they want it. Then, through trial and error, they create a home personality that keeps them safe, helps them avoid conflict, or just makes their parents smile and feel confident they're doing a good job.

Many moms and dads I speak to insist they tell their kids everything young boys and girls should hear. They insist on kindness, healthy habits, sharing, you name it. Yet, when I ask them how often those same parents do those things in front of their children and involve them, they give me a blank stare.

One mother came to me looking exhausted about her two sons, who seemed incapable of going two minutes without fighting. In addition, she had to deal with a custody battle with her ex-husband, who wanted more visitation rights yet left the boys alone whenever they went to his house. This led to endless arguments, often in front of their kids.

"I don't know what to do!" she told me, her head in her hands. "I know this is ugly. I know we're screwing them up, but I feel even worse if I don't fight for them. He's a terrible parent!"

Together we talked about what exactly she wanted to see from her ex-husband and then evaluated how that time alone affected her boys. Did they ever wander off, get into something they shouldn't, like a beer from the fridge? We made a list of demands for her ex. Then some brainstormed some things she could do to feel better about her kids being alone, should she lose in court.

I encouraged her to speak with her ex-husband as calmly as possible, despite her feelings about him. "Remember," I told her, "this is your chance to teach your kids how to solve a dispute. Think of it as a scene in a play, not a confrontation with the guy who left you." It took a while for her to get her emotions out of the equation, but soon she approached him with her list.

She wanted to know if he was going out, for the boys to always have a way to contact him, and for her ex to help pay for a First Aid class for the family. Then she asked him to make sure that the movies they watched at his house weren't too scary or explicit and that he always kiss them goodnight.

He took it badly and immediately started screaming, but she stood her ground. Seeing her refusal to argue eventually got her ex to calm down and start talking. Eventually, he agreed to her terms and realized how much time his kids spent alone.

The benefits extended to the kids. The boys still fought, but their mom noticed they also started trying to resolve their problems. As they got older, they valued a peaceful resolution over a massive, screaming fight.

After that, she and her family became much more open to alternative ways to model behavior and solve problems together.

Pro Tips

Working out our differences as a family can be a long journey and one I recommend you take with a professional, if possible. Otherwise, you may not end up in a good place. However, there are some things you can do with no help or extra degrees.

I want to walk you through some basics to get you started modeling good practices as a group and as individuals.

#1 Deep Breathing

Kids don't have the same breath control as adults, so they need a unique approach. First, they need to explore how the breath feels.

Start by playing outside. You can do a game of tag, some jump rope, whatever your kids like. Play with them. Then, after some fast-paced playtime, stop and ask them to let you "breathe" for a moment.

Use the opportunity to explain that breath changes as we play or rest. Let your little ones see you managing your breath for a few moments.

When you have a calm moment, get out some drawing paper or a stuffed animal, whatever works for your children, and try an exercise.

For the young artists, demonstrate how drawing a simple shape, like a triangle, can help you control your breath. For example, take three breaths to trace one side, hold for three on the next, then breathe out for three seconds as you close the shape. You can also do a square - breathe in for three seconds, hold the air in for three seconds, breathe out for three, keep the air out for three.

Another way is to have your child lie down and put a small stuffed animal on his or her belly. Ask your child to make the animal move using only their stomach, then go back down again. Another trick is to get out the bubble wand or pinwheel and practice blowing and breathing slowly. This one takes practice - bubbles are an enormous distraction!

If your child adores playing pretend, try imagining you're different animals and breathe accordingly. For example, a snake's breath makes a long hiss sound on the exhale. A whale needs a big deep breath, and then a big noisy exhale out of its blowhole. A bumblebee likes to smell flowers and then lets out a long "buzz."

#2 Get on the ground

A lot of parents forget that the world is enormous from the perspective of a little one. Most moms and dads I know look down at their children, but few of them get low and look their children in the eye.

Kids see everything differently once it's at eye level, their fears included. When the parents get down low on the ground and take the time to offer assurances, physical and verbal, it can move mountains.

Whenever your child feels angry, upset, or anxious, try sitting on her level. That might mean lying down on the floor, sitting in a chair for a child, or kneeling. Get your eyes down to the level of her eyes so you can offer a chance for her to hold your hand or get a friendly hug. Some children respond well to a gentle back rub or feeling someone play with their hair. Others just need a reassuring touch on their back or shoulder.

If you notice your child pulls away or seems tense with eye contact or touch, try a unique position. Sit or stand next to them to offer your support so you can be present without overpowering their personal space. Ask if they want to be alone for fifteen minutes, then circle back and see what's developed.

Don't push for a conversation until they're ready to talk. Your child may have a solid reason for staying silent for a moment. Trust that they understand you want to help.

#3 Ground with the senses

A great way to dispel some out-of-control anxiety is to practice grounding or use your physical sensations to get out of your mental state. This is great for adults as well, and I highly recommend it anytime you feel stressed.

Grounding is a simple matter of focusing on truths based on what you hear, smell, feel or taste in the moment. Even if you don't have any food nearby, you can always taste your tongue, a glass of water, or the surrounding air.

For kids, I have them start with their shoes. I ask them to wiggle their toes and focus on how their ten toes feel inside their socks and sneakers. Then we move up. I ask them to feel their skin without touching it, to feel their hair growing out of the roots.

After touching, I work with a smell. I try to challenge kids to find the distinct fragrances in the room instead of the overall scent. I ask them to smell the bookcase, the carpet, the furniture. This one also gets them breathing deeper and helps their muscles unwind.

Then on to taste. I ask them to tell me what their tongue tastes like at the moment, how the roof of their mouth tastes. If I can get away with giving them a mint or a small candy, I do, but only if it's appropriate.

Finally, I ask them to listen. Remember, it's hard to listen when we feel upset. Once we take a beat, listening becomes much more manageable. Listening to an environment provides a unique challenge. The longer we listen to the surrounding space, the further our hearing extends. Soon we hear the birds outside the window, the kids playing in the nearby park, the leaves of a nearby tree.

After we go through all the senses, we usually find a deep sense of calm. The exercise also reminds everyone to focus on what's happening at the moment, not what we imagine might happen.

Once you look for techniques to calm your child (and yourself) down, you'll begin to develop a list. My advice is to try something that you already like, or that feels similar to a hobby or interest you have.

You won't keep up a new habit if you feel bored by it or just hate it. If yoga isn't for you, don't force it. But, if it's something you always wanted to try, invite your child to join you for a brief part of the session.

Here's a shortlist of ideas to get you started:

- Make a Calm Down Jar. This is a jar filled with glitter and water that swirls around while your child watches, putting him or her in a meditative state in seconds.

- Make a vision board. Help you and your child imagine what amazing things await just over the horizon with a collection of images that represent your goals and the steps you can take to reach them.

- Write in a journal—my favorite. Journals are a great place to make lists of things we feel grateful for, something that distracts us, worries us, or do some sketches. Getting that noise out of our heads can help us focus for the rest of the day.

- Sing. Singing a song shifts our vibration. Even a sadder, slower song can change the way we feel.

- Blow out a candle. This can be another great way to practice slowing down our breath. Hold the candle close to your child to start, then move further and further away and encourage himto take a big, deep breath and blow it out.

- Watch fish in a pond or aquarium. Staring at fish can lower our heart rates and help us take a moment away from the stresses of the day. That's why you always see aquariums in hospitals!

- Visualize a beautiful place. Practicing visualization is a wonderful way to help the brain find a calm, therapeutic state. Think of your favorite vacation spot, a lovely garden, or your childhood home.

- Drink water. Dehydration does a ton of damage, including reduced brain function. Stopping to slowly sip a glass of water can also help us regulate our breathing and feel better about ourselves in a particular moment.

Make sure you practice whatever method you and your child choose together. If you only expect your son or daughter to calm down and relax without doing it yourself, you'll only keep the cycle of anxiety and stress in motion.

Don't worry about taking time to blow bubbles or draw pictures as you practice breath control. You'll benefit as much as your child. Probably more so.

The beauty of all of this is, you get to do it as a family and watch your children shift their state of mind. Put your judgment aside, sit in the grass, and be in the moment together. The joy at that moment will last a lifetime.

FINAL WORDS

This book rattled around in my head for years, long before I wrote it. Any time I mentioned the idea to a friend or colleague, I got plenty of encouragement, yet the idea of sitting down to write it froze me in place. So instead of sitting down at my desk, I stood and stared at the wall, wondering how exactly writers tackle the enormity of a book.

Luckily for me, I have a wonderful, supportive group of friends who saw my problem and named the real issue - I had the same anxiety I wanted to break down in my book. That hurt me twofold; it filled my head with doubts and venomous voices who insisted to me I could never successfully write, and it gave me imposter syndrome.

How could I write a book about leaving anxiety behind even as I continue to carry my own? When I first faced that truth, it crushed me. Was I really too scared to achieve my goals because I had the same problems I wanted to help others manage?

Once I had a handle on the thing holding me back, I could break it down with a good friend of mine whose job is to write books. She walked me through her research, outlining, and writing process, but more than anything, she let me in on a secret.

"No one feels confident that they're a good writer," she assured me. "And anyone who does often ends up writing garbage. Your doubt is proof that you want to do a good job. It means you're doing this for the right reasons."

With her love and a new perspective on the project holding me up, the blank page got a lot less scary. And once the first sentence came out of my head, the rest of it poured out so fast I could hardly keep up.

Writing this book filled me with so much joy. Every day I got to sit down and put all my time and effort into something that mattered to me. Every minute I researched new studies about anxiety and depression, I felt more confident that my book needed to exist and be out in the world.

But sharing it made me highly trepidatious. I couldn't believe how well my early readers received it and all the excellent advice they had for me to keep me going.

I met so many people who experience anxiety and have great ways to manage it. As I wrote it, I went from being an authority to a student and back again. This was an incredible journey, and I hope you got as much out of reading it as I did writing it.

A long list of people and situations inspired me, particularly my exposure to extreme cases of anxiety. Seeing anxiety at work in daily situations made me realize that these intense levels of fear kept the surrounding children from living the lives they wanted and prevented them from moving on from unpleasant experiences or sad moments. I learned everything I could about deep, paralyzing anxiety in hopes of better understanding the problem.

To my shock, I found that this persistent state also changed the brain's inner workings, a realization that made me dedicate hours of my day to helping kids and their families work out their anxiety. I'd always known that it was a destructive force, but seeing how it could prevent learning, change how a person's memory works, and even affect our general health made me take everything much more seriously.

After that, I had to let go of any lofty dreams of plucking anxiety out of someone's head and giving that person a perfect life. If only! No, I needed to see that anxiety never truly leaves us. Instead, it takes up residence in our minds and stays forever. But, once I learned how to change my relationship with my anxiety, I could help others reshape their attitudes about their anxious minds. We delved into ways to communicate our negative thoughts, name emotions literally and symbolically. Finally, we saw how fundamental changes helped everyone see themselves and their anxiety in a new light.

Some of the biggest surprises for me came in the small things parents say or ask their children that can heighten the problem. Many parents don't realize a small thing like a leading question can make a child feel enormous pressure to give the desired answer, even if it isn't true. Anxiety makes us work hard to make everyone around us feel happy, and others often feed into that need for approval, often without realizing it.

But, the small things can be whittled away with practice. One of my favorite things to do with families is picking apart how they communicate and help them build a new vocabulary that expresses curiosity and love for one another. It isn't easy; I get a lot of pushbacks, but it's all worth it when a child's or adult's emotional walls come down. Seeing family members connect authentically is a sight that consistently gets me inspired.

Helping others embrace, even come to love their anxiety is another massive highlight for me. Putting this problem that comes with so much stigma in a new light is an immense challenge, but I love to see people accept themselves, then come to love themselves, anxiety and all.

Accepting our anxious selves often makes us see how we judge and berate ourselves with intense clarity. It's a hard thing to take in, but once we do, we can change it. I know firsthand how powerful it can be to give ourselves kindness and extend it to our emotional selves. Once we love and be gentle with our anxious side, everything changes.

There's always a tightrope to walk with genuine acceptance. I want everyone to come to terms with their flaws, but I also have to be careful not to reinforce them. I hate to see someone see their future as dark and dreary thanks to an emotional problem. So instead, I work to help them respect their feelings and the emotions of others and work with them. No emotional issue should hold us back, but it deserves our attention, even if it's just for a moment.

If we can honor those darker, more (supposedly) negative parts of ourselves, I believe we can see them for what they are - a beautiful piece of ourselves. I know it feels strange to call anxiety beautiful, but I stand by that. I believe it.

A shift in our beliefs can change our lives, our entire world. Once we believe certain things about ourselves, our subconscious works overtime to make that thing true. I've seen it happen consistently. Some people call it manifesting, but I know it's a matter of letting go of limiting beliefs that keep us from getting the life we want.

The habit of spotting limiting beliefs helps us ferret them out and then dismantle them. I know so many people who say such awful things about themselves, and some do it so often they can't hear it anymore. We're so focused on being kind or at least polite with others, but we happily rip ourselves to shreds.

We like to think of this as living realistically, but nothing could be further from the truth. When we limit ourselves, our reality follows suit. Being realistic means recognizing that our thoughts and beliefs are powerful, and we need to honor that power.

I started this book with a lot of doubts and, of course, anxiety. I wondered if I would ever finish it and if it would ever make it into the hands of a reader. I let those worries keep me from starting while my belief that I could never write a book got bigger and louder.

Luckily for me, I had others around me who could easily point out the same issues with me that I often addressed in other people. So instead of focusing on the fact - that I had more than enough experience to write a book and could easily write for an hour a day, I let myself get stuck in the hamster wheel of emotion.

Once I grounded myself and focused on the evidence, not the feeling, I started typing.

I'm so glad I did.

If you enjoyed this book, please leave me a comment and a star rating on Amazon or Audible! Your reviews help others find this book. From the bottom of my heart, thank you!

PLEASE REVIEW MY BOOK YOU CAN
MAKE A DIFFERENCE

Enjoy this book? You can make a huge difference!

Reviews are the most powerful tool for authors when it comes to getting attention for our books! As much as I would love to have tons of money to throw at advertising I'm simply not there yet.

However... loyal readers such as yourself can make all the difference. Honest reviews of my book help bring them to the attention of other readers.

If you enjoyed my book I would be grateful if you would spend just five minutes leaving a review (as short or as long as you want it to be!) You can do so by simply clicking on the following link or typing it into your web browser.

https://www.amazon.com/review/create-review/?ie=UTF8&channel=glance-detail&asin=B098ZQL2M3

Thank you so much for your time!

JUST FOR YOU FOR BUYING MY BOOK

A FREE GIFT TO MY READERS...

The 5 Day Challenge to Improving Communication

Anyone can implement this challenge right away and instantly start improving the relationships in their lives!

Visit the link:

Elizabethnjacobs.com

ABOUT THE AUTHOR

Elizabeth N. Jacobs resides in Iowa with her husband, six year-old son and two dogs. She stays very busy between family life and running her own business. Elizabeth has always had a passion for children and a listening ear for those needing a confidant. This is Elizabeth's first book, though she has plans for several more all diving into children, marriage and relationships.

For more information:
Elizabeth@elizabethnjacobs.com

REFERENCES

This book is a culmination of my personal experiences, studies, and hard work. On top of that, I do a lot of reading and research to stay up to date on the latest research and takes on psychology, depression and anxiety.

For further reading, please check out the following studies and articles.

* *The*. (2019, July 9). Washington Post. https://www.washingtonpost.com/lifestyle/wellness/could-our-efforts-to-avoid-anxiety-only-be-making-it-worse/2019/07/09/df031504-91f5-11e9-aadb-74e6b2b46f6a_story.html

* *8 Ways to Teach Anxious Children to Cope With Their Feelings*. (n.d.). Verywell Family. Retrieved June

16, 2021, from https://www.verywellfamily.com/strategies-to-help-an-anxious-child-4177327

* *10 Easy Ways To Help Children Believe In Themselves.* (2018, August 29). HerFamily.Ie. https://www.herfamily.ie/parenting/10-easy-and-sweet-ways-that-you-can-help-children-believe-in-themselves-220395

A. (2020a, December 10).

* *How to Use Meditation for Teen Stress and Anxiety.* Health Essentials from Cleveland Clinic. https://health.clevelandclinic.org/how-to-use-meditation-for-teen-stress-and-anxiety/

* *Acceptance and Moving On.* (n.d.). Healthy Cells Magazine. Retrieved June 16, 2021, from http://www.healthycellsmagazine.com/articles/acceptance-and-moving-on

Agrawal, S. (n.d.).

* *Accept the Situation and Move On.* Thrive Global. Retrieved June 16, 2021, from https://thriveglobal.com/stories/accept-the-situation-and-move-on/

* *Anxiety and Depression in Children | CDC.* (2020a, December 2). Centers for Disease Control and Prevention. https://www.cdc.gov/childrensmentalhealth/depression.html#:%7E:text=When%20a%20child%20does%20not,types%20of%20anxiety%20disorders%20include

* *Anxiety and Depression in Children | CDC*. (2020b, December 2). Centers for Disease Control and Prevention. https://www.cdc.gov/childrensmentalhealth/depression.html#:%7E:text=Anxiety%20may%20present%20as%20fear,the%20symptoms%20can%20be%20missed.

* *Anxiety in Children*. (2020, August 6). Anxiety Canada. https://www.anxietycanada.com/learn-about-anxiety/anxiety-in-children/

* *Are There Potential Benefits to Having Anxiety?* (n.d.). Verywell Mind. Retrieved June 16, 2021, from https://www.verywellmind.com/benefits-of-anxiety-2584134#:%7E:text=Even%20though%20it%20may%20seem,to%20react%20faster%20to%20emergencies.

Arora, G. (2020, August 14).

* *Yoga For Anxiety: Do These 8 Yoga Poses Every Day To Curb Stress, Depression And Anxiety Symptoms*. NDTV.Com. https://www.ndtv.com/health/yoga-for-anxiety-do-these-8-yoga-poses-every-day-to-curb-stress-depression-and-anxiety-symptoms-2279418

Azarian, B. (n.d.).

* *How anxiety warps your perception*. BBC Future. Retrieved June 16, 2021, from https://www.bbc.com/future/article/20160928-how-anxiety-warps-your-perception

beyondblue - Healthy Families. (n.d.). Beyond Blue. Retrieved June 16, 2021, from https://healthyfamilies.beyondblue.org.au/age-6-12/mental-health-conditions-in-children/anxiety/strategies-to-support-anxious-children

biglifejournal.com. (n.d.-a).

* *4 Steps for Helping Your Child Set Effective Goals (Plus a Bonus Tip)*. Big Life Journal. Retrieved June 16, 2021, from https://biglifejournal.com/blogs/blog/goal-setting-for-kids#:%7E:text=Step%201%3A%20Let%20your%20child%20choose%20her%20%E2%80%9Cbig%20goal.,how%20you%20will%20address%20them.

biglifejournal.com. (n.d.-b).

* *7 Fun Goal-Setting Activities for Children*. Big Life Journal. Retrieved June 16, 2021, from https://biglifejournal.com/blogs/blog/5-fun-goal-setting-activities-children

Blog, F. (2020, July 23).

* *Leading Questions: Definitions, Types, and Examples*. Form PL. https://www.formpl.us/blog/leading-question

Buggy, P. (2017, December 21).

* *How to Overcome Limiting Beliefs and Access Your Potential*. Mindful Ambition. https://mindfulambition.net/overcome-limiting-beliefs/

Burnford, J. (2019, January 31).

* *Limiting Beliefs: What Are They And How Can You Overcome Them?* Forbes. https://www.forbes.com/sites/joyburnford/2019/01/30/limiting-beliefs-what-are-they-and-how-can-you-overcome-them/?sh=1045db826303

(c) Copyright skillsyouneed.com 2011–2021. (n.d.).

* *Benefits of Spending Time Alone | SkillsYouNeed*. Skills You Need. Retrieved June 16, 2021, from https://www.skillsyouneed.com/rhubarb/time-alone.html

Carlson, D. (2019, June 1).

* *Are your kids inheriting your fears? What parents can do to stop the cycle*. Chicagotribune.Com. https://www.chicagotribune.com/lifestyles/sc-fam-0414-inherited-fears-20150407-story.html

Carrie Shrier, Michigan State University Extension. (2021, March 17).

* *Young children learn by copying you!* MSU Extension. https://www.canr.msu.edu/news/young_children_learn_by_copying_you

Clear, J. (2020, February 4).

* *The Evolution of Anxiety: Why We Worry and What to Do About It*. James Clear. https://jamesclear.com/evolution-of-anxiety

Copland, S. (2018, February 14).

* *Anxiety is a way of life for Gen Y. In an insecure world, is it any surprise?* The Guardian. https://www.theguardian.com/society/commentisfree/2017/feb/25/anxiety-is-a-way-of-life-for-gen-y-in-an-insecure-world-is-it-any-surprise

Coyne, M. (2020, March 10).

* *Validation of children's feelings promotes positive mental health*. A Lust For Life - Irish Mental Health Charity in Ireland. https://www.alustforlife.com/tools/mental-health/validation-of-childrens-feelings-promotes-positive-mental-health

Cronkleton, E. (2018, June 6).

* *Yoga for Anxiety: 11 Poses to Try*. Healthline. https://www.healthline.com/health/anxiety/yoga-for-anxiety

Cultivate Confidence. (2021, January 20).

* *How To Raise Non-Judgmental Children - Cultivate Confidence*. Cultivate Confidence - Be Yourself. Be Confident. http://cultivateconfidence.com/raise-non-judgmental-children/

Curtin, M. (2020, February 6).

* *9 Ways to Get Rid of Anxiety in 5 Minutes or Less.* Inc.Com. https://www.inc.com/melanie-curtin/9-ways-to-get-rid-of-anxiety-in-5-minutes-or-less.html

Daniels, N. (2018, August 13).

* *Child Therapist's List of Top Childhood Fears by Age.* AT: Parenting Survival for All Ages. https://www.anxioustoddlers.com/worries-by-age/#.YG2ZcUgzbOQ

Davey, G. C. L. (2018, November 6).

* *Is There an Anxiety Epidemic?* Psychology Today. https://www.psychologytoday.com/us/blog/why-we-worry/201811/is-there-anxiety-epidemic

* *Deep Breathing Exercises for Kids.* (n.d.). Coping Skills for Kids. Retrieved June 16, 2021, from https://copingskillsforkids.com/deep-breathing-exercises-for-kids

* *Empowering children with positive beliefs.* (2019, January 4). Parenta.Com. https://www.parenta.com/2018/07/01/empowering-children-with-positive-beliefs/

Eurich, Q. (2020, November 17).

* *How to Stop Being a Victim of Your Own High Expectations.* Tiny Buddha. https://tinybuddha.com/

blog/how-to-stop-being-a-victim-of-your-own-high-expectations/

Fagell, P. L. (2017, May 9).

* *Eight ways parents can teach teens to be honest.* Washington Post. https://www.washingtonpost.com/news/parenting/wp/2017/05/09/8-ways-parents-can-teach-teens-to-be-honest/

Fairfax, R. (2017, July 11).

* *You Don't Have to Let Your Anxious Thoughts Control You.* Tiny Buddha. https://tinybuddha.com/blog/how-embracing-failure-can-help-us-deal-with-anxious-thoughts/

Firestone, L. (2018, July 3).

* *5 Truths about Anxiety to Help You Stay Present.* Psychology Today. https://www.psychologytoday.com/us/blog/compassion-matters/201807/5-truths-about-anxiety-help-you-stay-present

Fredricks, R. (n.d.).

* *How Exercise Can Reduce Anxiety - Information on Anxiety and Other Anxiety Related Mental Health Disorders.* Mental Help. Retrieved June 16, 2021, from https://www.mentalhelp.net/blogs/how-exercise-can-reduce-anxiety/

Fritscher, L. (2020, March 9).

* *Coping With Anticipatory Anxiety*. Verywell Mind. https://www.verywellmind.com/anticipatory-anxiety-2671554

G. (2020b, June 1).

* *37 techniques to calm an anxious child*. Motherly. https://www.mother.ly/child/37-techniques-to-calm-an-anxious-child

Gagne, C. (2020, September 10).

* *Age-by-age guide to getting your kid to talk to you*. Today's Parent. https://www.todaysparent.com/family/age-by-age-guide-to-getting-your-kid-to-talk/

Garey, J. (2020, April 8).

* *The Power of Mindfulness*. Child Mind Institute. https://childmind.org/article/the-power-of-mindfulness/

Gattuso, R. (2018, August 16).

* *The Unexpectedly Positive Attributes of Anxiety*. Talkspace. https://www.talkspace.com/blog/unexpected-positive-attributes-anxiety/

Gluskin, D. (2017; April 16).

* *The Power of Owning Your Story.* HuffPost. https://www.huffpost.com/entry/the-power-of-owning-your-_b_9702810

Guest Author for www.rtor.org. (2020, January 29).

* *Why Social Anxiety Disorder Is More And More Common in Our Society.* Resources To Recover. https://www.rtor.org/2020/01/29/why-social-anxiety-disorder-is-common-in-our-society/#:%7E:text=A%20negative%20style%20of%20parenting,common%20causes%20of%20social%20anxiety.

* Harvard Health. (2019, October 24). *Can exercise help treat anxiety?* https://www.health.harvard.edu/blog/can-exercise-help-treat-anxiety-2019102418096

* *Helping kids identify and express feelings.* (2021, January 19). Kids Helpline. https://kidshelpline.com.au/parents/issues/helping-kids-identify-and-express-feelings

* *Helping Kids When they are Scared.* (2017, November 22). Developing Minds. https://developingminds.net.au/blog/2017/6/27/helping-kids-when-they-are-scared

* *Helping Your Child Develop A Healthy Sense of Self Esteem.* (n.d.). HealthyChildren.Org. Retrieved June 16, 2021, from https://www.healthychildren.org/English/ages-stages/gradeschool/Pages/Helping-Your-Child-Develop-A-Healthy-Sense-of-Self-Esteem.aspx

Higgs, M. M. (2019, October 29).

* *Why You Should Find Time to Be Alone With Yourself.* The New York Times. https://www.nytimes.com/2019/10/28/smarter-living/the-benefits-of-being-alone.html

Holder, S. (2019, September 12).

* *Research Paper: Breaking the Chain of Self Limiting Beliefs in Children - Page 4 of 7.* International Coach Academy. https://coachcampus.com/coach-portfolios/research-papers/sheila-holder-breaking-the-chain-of-self-limiting-beliefs-in-children/4/

* *How Does Anxiety Affect the Brain? 4 Major Effects of Anxiety.* (2020, July 30). StoneRidge: Center for Brains. https://pronghornpsych.com/how-does-anxiety-affect-the-brain/

* *How Thoughts and Values May Affect Your Anxiety.* (n.d.). Verywell Mind. Retrieved June 16, 2021, from https://www.verywellmind.com/negative-thinking-patterns-and-beliefs-2584084

* *How to Model the Behavior You Want Your Child to Exhibit.* (n.d.). Verywell Family. Retrieved June 16, 2021, from https://www.verywellfamily.com/role-model-the-behavior-you-want-to-see-from-your-kids-1094785

Jain, R. (2017, September 7).

* *9 Things Every Parent with an Anxious Child Should Try*. HuffPost. https://www.huffpost.com/entry/9-things-every-parent-with-an-anxious-child-should-try_b_5651006

Jain, R. (2021, March 1).

* *50 Calm-Down Ideas to Try with Kids of All Ages*. GoZen! https://gozen.com/50-calm-down-ideas-to-try-with-kids-of-all-ages/

Katz, B. (2021, March 19).

* *How to Avoid Passing Anxiety on to Your Kids*. Child Mind Institute. https://childmind.org/article/how-to-avoid-passing-anxiety-on-to-your-kids/

Kazdin, A. C. R. (2009, January 27).

* *I Spy Daddy Giving Someone the Finger*. Slate Magazine. https://slate.com/human-interest/2009/01/your-kids-will-imitate-you-use-it-as-a-force-for-good.html

Kessler, D. P. (2018, March 15).

* *Why It Is So Important For Parents to Validate Their Children*. PsychAlive. https://www.psychalive.org/why-important-parents-validate-children/

Ledden, P. (2018, November 24).

* *How Beliefs are key to understanding our anxiety*. Abate Counselling. https://abatecounselling.ie/2018/

11/23/how-beliefs-are-key-to-understanding-our-anxiety/

Lindberg, S. (2018a, May 1).

* *15 Ways to Calm Yourself Down*. Healthline. https://www.healthline.com/health/how-to-calm-down

Lindberg, S. (2018b, November 27).

* *5 Ways Accepting Your Anxiety Can Make You More Powerful*. Healthline. https://www.healthline.com/health/how-anxiety-can-make-you-more-powerful

Martinelli, K. (2021, March 5).

* *How to Help Kids Who Are Too Hard on Themselves*. Child Mind Institute. https://childmind.org/article/how-to-help-kids-who-are-too-hard-on-themselves/

Matthews, D. C. (2020, December 10).

* *How to Identify Your Limiting Beliefs and Get Over Them*. Lifehack. https://www.lifehack.org/858652/limiting-beliefs#:%7E:text=Assess%20Your%20Behavior,underlying%20caus

e%20is%20limiting%20beliefs.

McDonald, B. (2019, April 30).

* *5 Ways to Help Your Kids Take Charge of Their Mental Health*. Better. https://better.net/life/health/ways-help-kids-take-charge-mental-health/

Meek, W. (2021, January 25).

* *5 Ways Anxiety Can Actually Bring Positivity to Your Life*. Verywell Mind. https://www.verywellmind.com/top-ways-anxiety-is-helpful-1393079

Mental Health Association of San Francisco. (2019, December 25).

* *Six Simple Habits That Defeat Anxiety*. https://www.mentalhealthsf.org/six-simple-habits-that-defeat-anxiety/

Monke, A. (2021, February 9).

* *10 Ways to Teach Kids to Calm Down*. Sunshine Parenting. https://sunshine-parenting.com/10-ways-teach-kids-calm/

Morin, A. (2017, October 5). \

* *Why It's So Hard To Change The Self-Limiting Beliefs You Learned During Childhood*. Forbes. https://www.forbes.com/sites/amymorin/2017/10/05/why-its-so-hard-to-change-the-self-limiting-beliefs-you-learned-during-childhood/?sh=906bbbd21851

Mortimer, S. (2020, October 27).

* *The limiting beliefs that keep you worrying*. Bristol Hypnotherapy. https://www.bristolhypnotherapy.co.uk/blog/2018/06/the-limiting-beliefs-that-keep-you.html

National Scientific Council on the Developing Child, Harvard University, & Center on the Developing Child. (2006).

* *Persistent Fear and Anxiety Can Affect Young Children's Learning and Development.* Harvard University. https://developingchild.harvard.edu/wp-content/uploads/2010/05/Persistent-Fear-and-Anxiety-Can-Affect-Young-Childrens-Learning-and-Development.pdf

Nelson, S. (2021, January 20).

* *How Accepting Anxiety Can Lead to Peace.* Tiny Buddha. https://tinybuddha.com/blog/how-accepting-anxiety-can-lead-to-peace/

Nichols, H. (2021, April 15).

* *How does yoga work?* Medical News Today. https://www.medicalnewstoday.com/articles/286745

Normal Childhood Fears (for Parents) - Nemours KidsHealth. (n.d.). Nemours Kids Health. Retrieved June 15, 2021, from https://kidshealth.org/en/parents/anxiety.html

Nutt, A. (2018, May 10).

* *Why kids and teens may face far more anxiety these days.* Washington Post. https://www.washingtonpost.com/news/to-your-health/wp/2018/05/10/why-kids-and-teens-may-face-far-more-anxiety-these-days/

Pas, M. (2020, March 16).

* *9 great ways to empower kids.* Parenting |. https://masandpas.com/9-ways-to-empower-your-kids/

Pelini, S. (2018, August 16).

* *3 things to ban from your kid's diet to calm anxiety and hyperactivity.* Raising-Independent-Kids. https://raising-independent-kids.com/3-things-ban-kids-diet-calm-anxiety-hyperactivity/

* *The Power of Acceptance: Stop Resisting and Find the Lesson.* (2021, May 27). Tiny Buddha. https://tinybuddha.com/blog/the-power-of-acceptance-stop-resisting-and-find-the-lesson/#:%7E:text=It%20helps%20you%20move%20from,what's%20going%20to%20happen%20next.&text=One%20thing%20that%20makes%20acceptance,why%20you're%20experiencing%20something.

Przeworski, A. (2014, May 30).

* *Facing Fears Without Pushing Your Child Over the Edge.* Psychology Today. https://www.psychologytoday.com/us/blog/dont-worry-mom/201405/facing-fears-without-pushing-your-child-over-the-edge

Richardson, B. (2015, December 2).

* *Ways To Help Your Child Express Their Feelings*. Lifehack. https://www.lifehack.org/337413/ways-help-your-child-express-their-feelings

Sanders, J. (2019, May 27).

* *10 Top Tips to Empower Kids*. Educate2Empower Publishing. https://e2epublishing.info/blog/2016/9/13/10-top-tips-to-empower-kids

Saviuc, L. D. (2020, August 18).

* *5 Healthy Ways To Let Go Of Self Judgment*. Purpose Fairy. https://www.purposefairy.com/91758/let-go-self-judgment/

Schwartz, S. (2020, May 12).

* *Why Sugar Can Make Your Kids More Anxious*. Happy Science Mom. http://happysciencemom.com/old/why-sugar-can-make-your-kids-more-anxious/

Stein, M. (2019, August 21).

* *Blog post - Thoughts are just Thoughts*. Understand Anxiety and Depression. https://adaa.org/learn-from-us/from-the-experts/blog-posts/consumer/thoughts-are-just-thoughts

strategy_llc. (2021, January 28).

* *4 Tips to Setting Realistic Expectations for Your Child*. The Confident Mom. https://theconfidentmom.com/09/mom-life/setting-realistic-expectations-for-your-child/

* *Stress in childhood*. (2021, June 9). Medline Plus. https://medlineplus.gov/ency/article/002059.htm

* Taylor, J. (2020, January 14). *What Are Your Biggest Limiting Beliefs?* Jane Taylor | Transition Coach | Engagement Coach | Wellbeing Coaching | Mindful Self-Compassion Coaching | Gold Coast | Mindfulness Teacher. https://www.habitsforwellbeing.com/what-are-your-biggest-limiting-beliefs/

* Team, B. A. S. (2020, August 26). *Is Anxiety Ruining Your Life? 9 Ways to Keep it at Bay*. Health Essentials from Cleveland Clinic. https://health.clevelandclinic.org/is-anxiety-ruling-your-life-try-9-ways-to-keep-it-at-bay/

* The Gottman Institute. (2020, June 11). *How to respect your child's emotions—even when you don't understand them*. Motherly. https://www.mother.ly/child/how-to-respect-your-childs-emotionseven-when-you-dont-understand-them

* *Tips to Manage Anxiety and Stress | Anxiety and Depression Association of America, ADAA*. (n.d.). ADAA. Retrieved June 16, 2021, from https://adaa.org/tips

* Treatment, C. (2020, February 25). *5 Ways Shame Can Shape Your Life*. Clearview Treatment Programs. https://www.clearviewtreatment.com/blog/5-ways-shame-can-shape-life/

* Tye, C. B. K. (2016, February 2). *7 Ways Anxiety Actually Works to Your Advantage*. GoodTherapy.Org Therapy Blog. https://www.goodtherapy.org/blog/7-ways-anxiety-actually-works-to-your-advantage-0202165

* Unger, M. (2016, September 30). *Why Are Kids so Anxious These Days?* Psychology Today. https://www.psychologytoday.com/us/blog/nurturing-resilience/201609/why-are-kids-so-anxious-these-days

* University of Delaware. (n.d.). *Self-Esteem Grows With Realistic Expectations | Cooperative Extension | University of Delaware*. Retrieved June 16, 2021, from https://www.udel.edu/academics/colleges/canr/cooperative-extension/fact-sheets/self-esteem-grows-with-realistic-expectations/

Vozza, S. (2018, July 16).

* *How to make your anxiety work for you instead of against you*. Fast Company. https://www.fastcompany.com/90179714/how-to-make-your-anxiety-work-for-you-instead-of-against-you

* *What Sugar and Caffeine Really Do to Your Anxious Child's Brain.* (n.d.). Anxiety Free Child. Retrieved June 16, 2021, from https://anxietyfreechild.com/sugar-caffeine-and-anxious-children/

* *Why 'bottling it up' can be harmful to your health | HCF.* (n.d.). HCF. Retrieved June 16, 2021, from https://www.hcf.com.au/health-agenda/body-mind/mental-health/downsides-to-always-being-positive

* *Why Is Anxiety So Common Today?* (2021, May 28). Mental Health Program at Banyan Treatment Centers. https://www.banyanmentalhealth.com/2019/03/11/why-is-anxiety-so-common/

* *Why Yoga May Ease Your Anxiety If You Have Panic Disorder.* (n.d.). Verywell Mind. Retrieved June 16, 2021, from https://www.verywellmind.com/yoga-for-panic-disorder-2584114

* *Why You Should Exercise to Relieve Symptoms of Mental Illness.* (n.d.). Verywell Mind. Retrieved June 16, 2021, from https://www.verywellmind.com/physical-exercise-for-panic-disorder-and-anxiety-2584094

* Williamson, T. (2021, June 14). *10 Breathing Exercises for Kids With Anxiety or Anger.* Mindfulmazing. https://www.mindfulmazing.com/10-breathing-exercises-for-kids-with-anxiety-or-anger/

* Wright, L. W. (2021, April 9). *Signs of anxiety in young kids*. Understood.Org. https://www.understood.org/en/friends-feelings/managing-feelings/stress-anxiety/anxiety-signs-young-children

Printed in Great Britain
by Amazon